Magnolia Gardens, *Charleston, South Carolina*

Henry E. Huntington Library Gardens, *San Marino, California*

Sterling Forest Gardens, *Tuxedo, New York*

PUBLIC GARDENS

AND ARBORETUMS

OF THE UNITED STATES

Text and Photographs by

MARTHA McMILLAN ROBERTS

With 10 full-color illustrations

Holt, Rinehart and Winston / New York

Ohme Gardens, *Wenatchee, Washington*

To Una Franklin Carter,
whose love of beauty
inspired this book.

PREFACE

Like the poet, every gardener and garden lover is caught up in the *mystique* of the creation of beauty. In this country, the tradition of gardens for pleasure began with the earliest English settlers. No sooner had they provided for the necessities of life than they started the cultivation of pleasure gardens. Even the pioneers in their push westward planted sunflowers, wild sweet peas, lupines, and wild roses. Since that time, the magnitude of American gardens and arboretums has become as vast as the expanse of our country. In no other land is there as great a divergence in climate and terrain and as great a variation in textures, forms, and plant life. Styles range from formal to informal, from the man-made garden to the man-and-nature-made, from the special garden to the garden of many specialities. Also, in no other country are there as many gardens and arboretums offering as broad and varied an educational program to the public.

When I began this book, I had visited only three of the public gardens in America. My knowledge of gardening was limited to that of an observer in an eighteenth-century town-house garden—watching things being planted and watching them grow. Neighbors came to admire, and at certain times the garden was open to the public. It was the beauty of this garden and the pleasure it gave to visitors that aroused my interest in public gardens in America. In the making of this book, I drove over thirty-five thousand miles, starting in the Deep South, moving up through the Southern

states, northward through New York and New England, across the Midwest into the tip of the Northwest, down the West coast of Southern California, and back across the Southwest. Even so, this is only a cross section, a sampling of our American gardens and arboretums. My visits to these lovely gardens opened up whole new vistas of beauty and pleasure for me. It was one of the richest experiences of my life and I hope that, you, in turn, will share my pleasure and enjoyment.

My gratitude goes to the directors, the horticulturalists, and gardeners who helped to make this book possible, with special appreciation for their enthusiasm in wanting their gardens shared by you and me alike. An indebtedness goes from all of us to the garden clubs throughout America for their ceaseless efforts in stimulating the interest of communities and of state and federal governments, and in aiding, through their donations and awards, the development of many of the public gardens and arboretums in the United States.

The arrangement of the material in the body of the book is alphabetical by the names of the gardens and arboretums. The index, however, groups them alphabetically by states, in order to provide easy reference according to geographical location. Since they are, in general, open daily to the public, I have made no attempt to include such factual information as hours or fees.

CONTENTS

PUBLIC GARDENS
AND ARBORETUMS
OF THE UNITED STATES

AIRLIE GARDENS

Wilmington, North Carolina

For half a century Airlie was a landmark in the social life of America. During the "Gilded Age," the Vanderbilts, Astors, Goulds, and Flaglers were frequent guests of the Pembroke Joneses at Airlie. Mr. Jones, former Chairman of the Board of the Atlantic Coast Line Railroad, bought the two thousand acres in the late 1890's as a hunting preserve and named it Airlie, after the Scottish home of his ancestors. The thirty-eight-room lodge, with a ballroom, conservatory, and banquet hall, designed by the noted architect, John Russell

Pope, was described by one guest as "the most perfect note of Italy in America." Topel, who in his youth had been undergardener to Kaiser Wilhelm, planned and supervised the development of the one-hundred-fifty-acre garden. Every known variety of azalea was planted. Mrs. Jones, kneeling on gunny sacking, planted some of them herself. After the death of her parents, in 1940, Mrs. John Russell Pope inherited Airlie. Eight years later, W. Albert Corbett, a Wilmington industrialist, bought the plantation and expanded the gardens.

The lodge was destroyed by fire in 1955, and Mr. Corbett's sons, who now own Airlie, replaced it with a colonial mansion.

The garden, on a bluff above Wrightsville Sound, is cooled by breezes coming over the tidal marshes from the not-too-distant Atlantic Ocean. Entered through a flower-embossed gate imported from France, the mile-long road leading to the gardens winds through a forest of native trees and shrubs. Masses of azaleas and camellias bank the lake, border the paths and lawns. Banksia roses hang from the bridges over the lake. From an open forest glade, carpeted with a seeming Oriental rug of dwarf Kurume azaleas divided by ribbons of emerald periwinkle, a jasmine-covered pergola marks the path down to the lake. In its setting of natural southern coastal beauty, Airlie is a masterpiece in rural landscaping.

3

THE ARNOLD ARBORETUM OF HARVARD UNIVERSITY

Jamaica Plain, Massachusetts

In 1872, with an endowment from James Arnold, a New Bedford merchant, and a gift of one hundred twenty-five acres of farmland from Benjamin Bussey of Roxbury, Harvard University established the Arnold Arboretum. Some ten years later, at the suggestion of landscape architect Frederick Law Olmsted, the City of Boston was given title to the land. In turn, the city leased it back to Harvard for nine hundred ninety-nine years at one dollar a year.

During his fifty-four years as the first director, Charles Sprague Sargent set ". . . the study of the world's vegetation" as the arboretum's aim. Its work has been international as well as national in scope. Thousands of exotic plants have been collected from European and Asiatic countries, the Far East, and Africa from the equator south. There is an extensive horticultural library and a large herbarium. Members of the staff have made

4

important scientific studies and introduced plants of both ornamental and scientific value.

The paths and roads wind around the two hundred sixty-five acres of hilly terrain. Beginning with the first bloom of the Oriental witch hazel and ending with the turn of the leaves, there are flowers or fruit from early spring until late fall. In the spring, the blooming of the Oriental cherries, azaleas, and crab apples, of dogwood, lilac, and magnolia, is followed by that of mountain laurel, rhododendron, and mock orange. In summer, the mimosa, spirea, buttonbush, and tamarisk bloom is followed by Franklinia and sweet autumn clematis. In their varying hues of green, the hemlocks, spruces, junipers, and pines add color to the arbo-

retum throughout the year. Today, its living collection includes six thousand different kinds of trees, shrubs, and vines from all parts of the North Temperate Zone.

5

ASTICOU GARDENS

Northeast Harbor, Maine

Set at the edge of the inlet, Northeast Harbor, the gardens have a view of the nearby mountains and the Atlantic Ocean. Crushed red granite paths meander along a stream and around a lake with pond lilies and grasses growing at the edge of its pebbled beaches. Cedar, pine, hemlock, maple, spruce, white birch, and ash shade the woodland paths bordered by native ground covers of lambkill, bayberry, and bunchberry. Azaleas, rhododendrons, Japanese crab apples, and red maples lend color to the greens. Native stone—jasper and red and gray granite—has been used to carry out the symbolism of mountains. A garden with rocks resting on raked waves of sand, representing the islands in the ocean, is patterned after one at the Zen temple in Kyoto.

The symbolism inherent in Japanese gardens has been achieved at the Asticou Gardens with the natural setting and the native materials of Maine. Mr. Charles Savage, owner of the gardens, created and designed them himself. Many of the plants were formerly in the Reef Point Gardens of the noted landscape architect Beatrix Farrand at Bar Harbor, which **were dismantled** upon her death in 1959.

BELLINGRATH GARDENS

Mobile, Alabama

Combining natural and man-made beauty, Bellingrath is often referred to as the "charm spot of the Deep South." The estate, created by Mr. and Mrs. Walter Bellingrath, dates back to 1917 when Mr. Bellingrath built a fishing lodge on the banks of the Isle-aux-Oies River some twenty miles south of Mobile. A civic, religious, and cultural leader, "Mr. Bell," as he was often called, used the place for entertaining. Surrounded by a wilderness of oaks, pines, and semitropical plants, the lodge and its grounds became a gardener's challenge to its owners. The present-day gardens and Renaissance house were planned by the famous landscape designer and architect, George B. Rogers, in 1927. The sixty-acre garden was opened to the public in 1932, and the house, with the Bessie Morse Bellingrath Collection of antiques, was opened upon the death of Mr. Bellingrath in 1955.

Through wrought-iron gates, once owned by the first governor of Louisiana, one enters on paths that lead through a rose garden, across the "Great Lawn" banked by flowers, shrubs, and trees, around pools and fountains, through the formal gardens and terraces surrounding the house, along the banks of the river, down through the terraced rock garden, around Mirror Lake, and up the hillside to the camellia arboretum. The garden's first burst of color comes early in February with the blooming of hundreds of azaleas and camellias, followed by hyacinths, lilies, daffodils, dogwood, and mountain laurel. Roses and calla lilies, Japanese, Easter, and day lilies bloom throughout May and June. Summer brings the flowering of the crape myrtle and lantana and the green of many tropical-foliage plants, followed by the fall display of chrysanthemums. In October's Indian summer the fall camellias and the Belgian hybrid azaleas begin their winter bloom. As Mr. Bell once said, "There is no season here in the Garden. We have beauty every day of the year"

9

BERKELEY
ROSE GARDEN
Berkeley, California

On a hillside above San Francisco Bay, the Berkeley Rose Garden has a view westward across the water to the Golden Gate. Originally, the rocky hillside was covered by weed and brush. During the years 1933–37, the CWA and the WPA cleared the land and constructed the present garden. Designed as a rock-terraced amphitheater, the four acres in Codornices Park were planted and developed under the supervision of the Berkeley Parks Department. Today, it is a demonstration garden of the American Rose Society.

Located on Scenic View Drive, in the heart of the beautiful Cragmont residential section, its blooming season spans the months from April until mid-October. With color varying from terrace to terrace, the garden is unique in its display. On the upper terraces, beds of red roses deepen into tones of copper. Masses of climbing red roses cover a redwood pergola stretching across one terrace. Below the pergola, terraces of multi-colors —flame, yellow and pink—fade into beds of white roses on the lower terraces. Old-fashioned roses, as well as the latest-known varieties, are planted throughout. Bordered by junipers on the slopes and surrounded by stately Italian cypresses, the garden has the flavor of an Old World one sitting high on the cliffs above the Mediterranean.

10

BERKSHIRE
GARDEN CENTER

Stockbridge,

Massachusetts

In the beginning, the idea for the Berkshire Garden Center was a humble and modest one. With eight and a half acres of land and a cottage given by Mr. and Mrs. Bernhard Hoffmann in 1934, the members of the Lenox Garden Club, together with five other Berkshire County Garden Clubs, announced: "It is proposed to start a Garden Center in Berkshire County for a year's trial." Immediately, the Garden Club Federation of Massachusetts notified the Founders that they would make their next year's pilgrimage to the Center. With this enthusiastic response, the Founders decided to make the Center a clearinghouse for garden information and horticultural experiment. Landscape architect Edward Belches, who was Horticultural Chairman of the Center for many years, drew up the master plan of the garden. With donations of money and plant materials and with the help of many individuals and garden clubs, the Center has succeeded in fulfilling

12

its aim. Any day of the week, any month of the year, there are a round of activities—lectures, flower and vegetable shows, exhibits, workshops, and nature walks for children. The Harvest Festival—where jams, jellies, herbs, canned fruits and vegetables, homemade bread and cakes, plants and dried-flower arrangements are on sale—has become an annual fete. For its contribution to the community throughout its twenty-seven years, the Center has won awards from the National Council of State Garden Clubs, the Massachusetts Horticultural Society, the Garden Club of New Jersey, and the Garden Club Federation of Massachusetts.

Nestled in a valley of the Berkshires, northwest of Stockbridge, the Center is open throughout the growing season. Sloping down from the cottage which houses the Center's horticultural library, the green lawn is bordered by beds of annuals and perennials backed by a dry wall enhanced by native shrubbery and rock plants. The Herb Garden, with culinary and medicinal plants, edges on the Dwarf Apple Orchard and Vineyard. In the garden's sun-heated pit, tender pot plants are stored, and its lath house shelters an ever-changing display of flowering plants. For all who love beauty in nature, the Center is a common gathering place.

13

"BILTMORE"

Asheville, North Carolina

When young George Vanderbilt, grandson of Commodore Cornelius Vanderbilt, sat rocking on the porch of the old Battery Park Hotel one day in the late nineteenth century, he studied the view of the mountains beyond, and decided that this was the setting he wanted for his house. Soon afterward, he purchased one hundred and twenty-five thousand acres of woodland, farmland, and forested mountains on the outskirts of Asheville. In 1890, he consulted his friend, the well-known architect Richard Morris Hunt, who drew up plans for a house of the French Renaissance period patterned after the châteaux at Blois and Chambord. With skilled workmen brought from France, England, Italy, and Egypt, the two-hundred-fifty-room house took five years to complete. Called "Biltmore," the estate derives its name from Bilde, the Netherlands town of Mr. Vanderbilt's forebears, and "more" from the English moor of rolling upland country. Frederick Law Olmstead, the noted landscape architect, designed the gardens, and for sixty years afterward, Chauncey Beadle, Superintendent of Biltmore, collected plants, trees, and shrubs from all parts of the world. Reforestation was under the direction of Gifford Pinchot and his supervisor, Dr. C. A. Schenck, who, in 1898, founded the first school of forestry in the United States at Biltmore. Mrs. Vanderbilt, upon the death of her husband in 1914, gave more than one hundred thousand acres of the forest to the government. Today this land forms the nucleus of the Pisgah National Forest.

The grounds of the estate, and the house with its rare collection of European furniture, tapestries, paintings, and porcelains, were opened to the public in 1930 by George Vanderbilt's grandson, George Cecil.

In the natural setting of the Blue Ridge Mountains, Biltmore's twelve thousand acres include pastures, meadows, streams, and woodlands of conifers, hemlocks, hollies, magnolias, tulip trees, mountain laurel, and rhododendron. Five formal gardens cover thirty-five acres. The Azalea Garden is the only complete collection of native American types in the world. Formal in design, the Italian, Shrub, Rose, and Spring gardens have an array of flowers from late April until late October. With an unsurpassed variety of exotic and native flora, Biltmore is one of the horticultural showplaces of the world.

THE BISHOP'S GARDEN

Washington Cathedral,

Washington, D.C.

For centuries, bishops' gardens have been places of beauty and tranquility, but unlike most, the Bishop's Garden at the National Cathedral is open to the public. At first the inspiration of the late Mrs. Florence Bratenahl, the garden became a reality in 1928, with the support of many persons. Mrs. Bratenahl, by studying worn tapestries, illuminated manuscripts, records of medieval gardens, and woodcuts, worked out the design and, with fellow members of the All Hallows Guild of the Cathedral, sought contributions. Through donations from individuals and the garden clubs of Cleveland, Dayton, Wilmington, Rye, North Shore, and Millbrook, they obtained trees, plants, shrubs, and many old stone carvings.

Sitting on a terraced slope beneath the unfinished spires of the Cathedral, Bishop's Garden is entered through an eight-hundred-year-old Norman Arch set in an ivy- and rose-covered stone wall. The box-bordered winding paths, made of stones from George Washington's Aquia Creek quarry, lead through the herb garden with a ninth-century font, through the rose garden with a twelfth-century Wayside Cross and a sundial, to the Memory Garden watched over by Saint Fiacre, the Patron Saint of Gardens. Extending the length of the garden, Yew Walk leads up the old stone steps taken from "Abingdon," the home of Nelly Custis, to the Garden House, shaded by honey locust. With a twelfth-century Norman Court, protected by cedars of Lebanon from the Holy Land, and walls covered by ivy from Canterbury Cathedral, Bishop's is a garden of "The Ages."

17

ALFRED E. BOERNER
BOTANICAL GARDEN

Hales Corner, Wisconsin

Set on the crest of a hill in Whitnall Park, the garden is dedicated to the growing of every tree, flower, and shrub native to Wisconsin. Appropriately named, the garden and park itself are a living memory to two men—the late Alfred E. Boerner, former park landscape architect and head of the Park Department, and the late Charles B. Whitnall, a member of the Park Commission—who originated the idea. They induced the Milwaukee County Park Commission to buy six hundred fifty-five acres of farmland in 1930 and develop four hundred fifty of those acres as an arboretum and botanical garden. The garden was constructed by the CCC and WPA in 1932 and opened to the public in 1939. Under the direction of the Park Commission, the garden maintains a library and

18

information center. Classes in horticulture, lectures, art exhibits, and flower shows are staged in the administration building, and outdoor clinics are held in the spring and fall. A scientific research program is carried on to study the hardiness of native and exotic plants in the region. It is the test garden for All-American Rose Selections, All-American Mum Selections, and the American Hemerocallis Society.

In a rolling landscape, the garden is surrounded by wooded hillsides, lakes, and spring-fed brooks. Within the terraces and malls, the rock garden, perennial and tulip gardens, rose and herb gardens, along with the collections of lilac and dogwood, of irises, chrysanthemums, daylilies, and tree peonies, cover a blooming season from April until mid-October. The Nature and Hiking trails lead through a forest of shagbark hickory, old hawthorne, white and red oak, silver maple, white ash, hemlock, pine, white cedar, and larch. The marshes, stream banks, meadows, and lagoon borders are a wonderland for bird and nature study at any time of the year.

19

BOSTON PUBLIC GARDEN

Boston, Massachusetts

In a city steeped in culture from the time of its beginning as the capital of the Commonwealth of Massachusetts, the Boston Public Garden takes its place among the cultural landmarks. In 1859, Mr. Horace Gray and a few friends interested in horticulture decided to establish a public garden for the people of Boston. They leased an old circus building at Beacon and Charles Streets from the city and converted it into a conservatory for birds and plants. In the beginning, the western boundary of the conservatory edged the muddy banks of the Charles River, but soon after the opening, the City itself filled in the land, planted the surrounding grounds, and made it an outdoor

20

public garden. Then a part of Boston Common, the garden was destroyed by a fire sweeping down through the seven old ropewalks and clearing the land. It was rebuilt as a separate garden, divided from the Common by Charles Street. Under the supervision of the Park Department, it was replanted in 1872 and its twenty-four acres were enclosed by an iron fence.

Near the gates of the main entrance, a life-sized statue of Edward Everett Hale, clergyman, philanthropist, and author of *A Man Without a Country*, faces, across the garden, a statue of George Washington, "The Father of Our Country." Beds of annuals and perennials bordering the walks add a brilliance of color to the vast expanse of lawn. American, Scottish, and English elms, silver maples, weeping willows, and sycamores, white ash, weeping beech, and catalpa, provide shade. The ducks gliding along the unrippled surface of the lake set a leisurely pace for the boat rides through the garden.

SILVER MOON
CLIMBER
INTRODUCED 1910
BROOKLYN BOTANIC GARDEN

22

BROOKLYN BOTANIC GARDEN

Brooklyn, New York

As a place of solitude and beauty in the heart of a city, the Brooklyn Botanic Garden serves one of the largest metropolitan communities in America. Established in 1911 as a division of the Brooklyn Institute of Arts and Sciences, its fifty acres are owned and maintained by the City of New York. Throughout the years, Brooklyn Botanic has contributed to the educational program of the community. In co-operation with the public schools, classes in horticulture and plant lore have become an integral part of the garden's activities. Scientific research by members of the staff has added to the knowledge of plants and their culture. Through grants and donations, fellowships are given for research and for training in socially slanted botany and horticulture. The horticultural library is one of the most outstanding in the country. With one of the largest living plant collections in the world, the garden is open to the public every day of the year.

Surrounded by a border of trees that muffle the hum of the city, the garden is really many in one. The tree-shaded sloping paths wind through wooded areas, along streams, across lawns of crocuses and daffodils, and through the Rock Garden, the Rose and Children's Garden, the Japanese Garden, the Shakespearian Garden, the Herb, Wildflower, and Iris gardens, and the Garden of Fragrance created for the blind. In front of the conservatory, housing desert and tropical plants, the reflecting pool is afloat with lotus and water lilies. Famous for the spring flowering of Japanese cherries, azaleas, lilacs, dogwoods, and flowering crab apples the garden has bloom at all seasons. With beauty to satisfy all tastes, Brooklyn Botanic is an essential part of the community.

23

CITY PARK

New Orleans, Louisiana

The huge oak in City Park is dedicated to the
park's benefactor, John McDonough, a handsome
Baltimorean who moved to New Orleans in 1800.
For many years he was socially prominent and
financially prosperous. Later, when an unfortunate
love affair drove him across the river, he became
a social recluse but continued his interest in business affairs to the extent that he was known as
"McDonough the Miser." When he died in 1850,
New Orleans was startled to learn that he had
left the city his vast estate, asking in return only
that "the little children shall sometimes come and

24

plant a few flowers above my grave." In 1891, the Commissioners of the Park Department started to develop eighty-five acres of John McDonough's land. With funds from the estate, they purchased adjoining land and increased the park to its present fifteen hundred acres.

The entrance, through Monteleone Gate, is set off by a huge floral clock, and the winding boulevards are flanked by spreading oaks and towering palms. Deep within the park, the Rose Garden, with new and old-fashioned varieties, is bordered by gardenias; the Azalea Garden is enclosed by a hedge of yaupon holly; the Camellia Garden is shaded in part by the Dueling Oak. The greenhouses have a year-round display of subtropical plants and seasonal displays of flowering plants. Oaks, hackberry, crape myrtle, pine, camphor, cedar, sequoia, bald cypress, and bamboo are among the twenty-two thousand trees casting their shadows on the broad lawns. Ducks and swans float easily along on the surface of the seventeen miles of lagoons.

THE GARDENS OF
THE CLEVELAND MUSEUM
OF ART

Cleveland, Ohio

The Cleveland Museum's belief in the complementary relationship between sculpture and living forms out of doors has made its garden an extension of its galleries. Enclosed by the museum itself, the sculpture Court, opened in the spring of 1958, was the joint work of landscape architect Gilmore Clarke, William Strong—who designed the planting—and John Teare—who supervised its installation.

It is paved with colorful crab-orchard flagging, and the steps leading into it are gray granite. Honey locust and red oak cast their shadows over the ground covers of dwarf yew, English ivy, and Japanese holly in the beds dividing the courtyard. In the open sunny areas, varieties of heath and heather flower on warm winter days. On the south side of the court the large garden pool is backed by rhododendron, Japanese holly, northern bayberry, and dwarf cherry laurel. On the north side of the court, southern way myrtle, azaleas, American gallberries, evergreen barberries, and rhododendrons are shaded by flowering dogwoods and magnolias. Throughout the court, bronze and stone sculptures by Rodin, Kolbe, Lipchitz, and McVey are integrated with the plantings.

27

THE CLOISTERS

Fort Tryon Park, New York, New York

On a rock ledge high above the busy Hudson River, with a view of the sweep of the George Washington Bridge. The Cloisters is a living reconstruction of the monasteries of the Middle Ages. In 1925 John D. Rockefeller, Jr., gave the fabulous George Grey Barnard collection of medieval sculpture and architectural materials to the Metropolitan Museum of Art. Five years later, he donated the land for Fort Tryon Park to the City of New York with the stipulation that the northern hilltop should be reserved for the construction of The Cloisters. Designed by Charles Collens, the plans were taken from the cloisters of five monasteries in France dating from the twelfth through the fifteenth centuries. Since the opening in 1938, new acquisitions of paintings, sculpture, tapestries, and architectural elements have been procured by private donations and through purchase.

28

The gardens of the old monasteries were not only places of beauty for contemplation, but also practical gardens, supplying fruits, vegetables, seasoning and medicinal herbs. On a sunny terrace above the river, the garden of the Bonnefant Cloister is based on similar ones in paintings, tapestries, and illuminated manuscripts, as well as on a surviving list of herbs which Charlemagne had had grown in the imperial gardens in 812 A.D. Kitchen herbs—thyme, sage, marjoram, and parsley—and medicinal herbs—camomile, stramonium, agrimony, betony, and lady's-mantle—are surrounded by candytuft, pinks, bleeding heart, damask roses, and lilies, and shaded by pear and apple trees. The Cuxa Cloister has been designed as an example of a garden for contemplation and prayer. Around its fountain from Saint-Genis-des-Fontaines, the spring-blooming plants flower beneath the apple trees. In all its beauty, The Cloisters brings to the present one of the finest collections of art work from the past.

THE COLONIAL GARDEN

Elizabethtown, New York

Inspired by the beauty of the gardens of the early Virginia settlers and their English forebears, the Essex County Historical Society, in 1955, added a formal colonial garden to their museum. Its ground plan is designed after the sunken garden of Henry VIII at Hampton Court. A lead-embossed cistern and a dolphin fountain from Barn Hill in Surrey and a sundial from Kirkby Hall in Leicester emphasize the English tradition. Adapting the pattern of the gardens of Williamsburg, flower beds are edged with brick, the gravel paths are laid out in eighteenth-century style, the summer house is similar to those of 1760, and the ironwork was forged by craftsmen at contemporary Williamsburg.

With a view of the Adirondacks, the garden is bordered on two sides by clipped hedges. At one end, the gate of the white picket fence is copied from historic Pepperell House in Kittery, Maine; at the other end the brick wall, laid in Flemish bond, is copied from the wall surrounding the Capitol at Williamsburg. Plantings are typical of those in colonial Virginia and in eighteenth-century northern gardens. From spring until fall the garden is alive with the color of phlox, cineraria, verbena, dwarf cockscomb, peony, bleeding heart, heliotrope, delphinium, lobelia; of marigolds, pink and lavender petunias, forget-me-nots, tuberous begonias, and madonna and Japanese lilies. Lilac, Japanese quince, juniper, hemlock, spruce, willow, and red-stem dogwood surround the garden. The paths of the Wild Flower Garden lead through woodlands of cucumber root, wood anemone, wild geranium, bloodroot, shooting star, May apple, red and white baneberry, wood sorrel, St. John's-wort, mallow, Canada and wood lilies.

THE GARDENS OF
COLONIAL WILLIAMSBURG

Williamsburg, Virginia

In the English tradition, the early Virginia colonists were enthusiastic gardeners, and as soon as they had provided for necessities, they planted pleasure gardens. At Williamsburg, their original capital, the colonial period has been re-created in authentic detail in order "that the future may learn from the past." The restoration was the idea of the late Reverend W. A. R. Goodwin, pastor of the old Burton Parish Church, and was accomplished by Colonial Williamsburg, Inc., a nonprofit corporation established by John D. Rockefeller, Jr. The work was begun in 1917 with the acquisition of one colonial house; since then almost five hundred buildings have been restored or reconstructed.

Eighty acres of gardens and greens, ranging from a forty-by-fifty-foot herb garden to the ten-acre garden of Governor's Palace, have been redesigned and landscaped. In their work, the landscape architects relied on old manuscripts, excavations, and studies of surviving evidence. Formal in design, the ninety gardens are patterned in straight lines and sharp corners to conform to the symmetrical character of colonial architecture. Many are laid out like miniature plantations, with a kitchen garden and a flower garden linked by marl or brick paths to the house and outbuildings. In eighteenth-century fashion, evergreens are used to form geometric patterns with colorful annuals and bulbs to provide contrast. The magnificent Palace gardens consist of a yaupon-holly maze imitative of Hampton Court, an orchard with espaliered trees, a long beech arbor, terrace gardens, and a kitchen garden. Circular shaped tree-boxwoods in the garden of Elkanah Deane, once a prosperous coachmaker, and the setting-hen boxwood in the Bryan garden are fine examples of topiary. American elms, oaks, paper mulberries, John Custis yews, pecans, hackberries, catalpas, and osage oranges lend dignity to the lawns and give a living sense of continuity with the past.

CORKSCREW SWAMP
SANCTUARY

Immokalee, Florida

At the northern tip of Big Cypress Swamp, this country's largest remaining stand of bald cypress has been preserved by the National Audubon Society. These trees are the oldest in eastern North America, and many had been standing for over two centuries when Columbus arrived. In 1954, as loggers' saws drew near to this stand of cypress, the Audubon Society appealed for donations to preserve it. J. Arthur Curry, President of the Lee Tidewater Cypress Company, gave six hundred forty acres for the sanctuary, and from other gifts the Society was able to purchase an additional twenty-eight hundred and eighty acres of cypress land. For a nominal sum they leased another thirty-two hundred acres of the surrounding land of pine and small cypress trees. A program of conservation has saved rare and exotic plants. A natural environment for the nesting and breeding of native birds has been preserved, and thousands of subtropical and migrating birds find haven in its lakes and ponds.

A cypress boardwalk winds through pine flatwoods, across lakes and ponds covered with water lettuce, back into the heart of the cypress swamp. The rays of the warm sun are diffused by heavy streamers of Spanish moss hanging from the towering one-hundred-twenty to one-hundred-thirty-foot trees. Nests of wood storks and white ibis make a frosted crown in their tops. Clumps of night-smelling orchids, onion and cigar orchids, jingle-bell and shell orchids nestle in the branches. Pink, green, and white lichens pattern the bark. Fire flags and swamp lilies, arrowhead and wampee, and ferns of many varieties cover the patches of earth in the swamp. Alligators and water moccasins lazily sun themselves on moss-covered logs. In this primeval forest the mysteries of nature reflect themselves in beauty.

GARDENS OF CRANBROOK

Bloomfield Hills, Michigan

Among rolling hills, the church, three schools, institute of science, and art academy of Cranbrook are set amid woodlands, tree-shaded lawns, streams, formal gardens, and lakes. A foundation since 1927, Cranbrook dates back to 1904. When other Detroiters were riding the interurban electric cars to nearby lakeshore summer resorts, George C. Booth, a Detroit newspaper publisher, and his wife, Ellen Scripps Booth, risked driving over dusty and rutted roads in their Winton to explore the countryside. On one such trip they decided on Bloomfield Hills as a summer retreat, and bought three hundred acres of old farmland

36

from the naturalist, Samuel Alexander, for whom a species of oak is named. They used his small house as a summer residence while building their larger one. On its completion in 1908, they pioneered in year-round country living. They named the estate Cranbrook, after the Kentish village from which Mr. Booth's father, a clergyman, had emigrated. In 1918, when Bloomfield Hills began to expand, Mr. Booth built a meeting house on his property. It served as a place for community gatherings, a school for neighborhood children, and a church, where his father, Henry Wood Booth, conducted services. Eight years later the meeting house became Christ Church Cranbrook. From this, Cranbrook grew to the educational and cultural center it is today.

Throughout the grounds, beds of flowering plants adorn the lawns and terraces and border the walks. In the spring, flowering cherries and crab apples add a contrasting sparkle to the hues of the evergreens. Fountains and pools reflect the tall oaks, elms, and maples. The formal gardens, with sculptures by Carl Milles, surround the Art Academy designed by the late Eliel Saarinen, both former artists-in-residence at Cranbrook. On one side of the academy loggia, annuals reflect their color in Milles's "Orpheus Fountain"; on the other side, colorful rose borders are mirrored in a pool with Milles's "Tritons" and "Europa and the Bull." Cranbrook House itself is surrounded by circular terraces overlooking Kingswood Lake, formal gardens with pools, woodlands of pines and cedars, streams, and waterfalls.

THE BAYARD CUTTING ARBORETUM

Great River, Long Island, New York

In 1952, Mrs. Bayard James donated the former Cutting summer estate, "Westbrook," to the Long Island State Park Commission in memory of her father, William Bayard Cutting. The property, on the West Brook of the Connetquot River, had been a part of the Nicholl Patent purchased from the Indian tribe, Sachem of Connetquot. In 1881, Mr. Cutting bought six hundred fifty-three acres of the land and engaged Charles Haight as the architect for his Elizabethan house. Six years later, with the help of Frederick Law Olmsted, Mr. Cutting planned the arboretum and ordered from England the first trees for the Pinetum. A civic and business leader and philanthropist, he stated that the purpose of the arboretum was "to provide an oasis of beauty and quiet for the pleasure of those who delight in outdoor beauty." Endowed by Mrs. Cutting, the arboretum is today, as it was yesterday, an "oasis of beauty." The Cutting home houses the library and is used as a center for nature-study groups.

The arboretum has a wide variety of nature walks. Bordered by mass plantings of rhododendron and azalea, the Rhododendron Walk leads through woodlands of native laurel, andromedas, dogwood, native oaks, and holly. Along the riverbank, the Swamp Cypress Walk leads to the Bird Watchers' Walk. Meandering through woodlands and fields, the walk provides cover, nesting places, and food for numerous inland and shore birds. The Wild Flower Walk winds through tidewater meadows and marshes, along streams and ponds, through native woodlands. The imaginative planning of many decades makes the arboretum as beautiful in winter snow as in summer blossom.

THE DAWES ARBORETUM

Newark, Ohio

Few American countrysides lend themselves more fittingly to arboretum planting than the rolling green hills of south-central Ohio. Beman G. Dawes, founder of the Pure Oil Company and brother of Charles G. Dawes, former Vice President of the United States, had a hobby of studying the trees of his native Ohio. In 1917, he bought three hundred twenty-five acres south of Newark, primarily because of a beautiful grove of sugar maples in front of the house. He began the development of the property by transplanting fifty large sugar maples from the woodlands to the grove. Five years later, under his direction thirty thousand trees were added. A series of tree dedications began at the arboretum in 1927, with Hon. James M. Cox, then Governor of Ohio, dedicating the first. Since then, sixty-four trees in the arboretum have been dedicated and bear such famous names as Rear Admiral Richard E. Byrd, Admiral William F. Halsey, heavyweight boxing champion Gene Tunney, aviator Wiley Post, golfer Bobby Jones, and inventor Orville Wright. When Mr. Dawes donated the arboretum to the public in 1929, General John J. Pershing dedicated one of the trees in elm row, which now bears his name. Since its opening, the arboretum has been expanded to five hundred twenty-five acres, with particular emphasis on the culture of trees and shrubs hardy in the climate of Ohio.

Throughout the arboretum there are trees and shrubs from several continents and many climates, including specimens from Japan, Australia, Korea, China, Switzerland, Great Britain, and Italy. Formal avenues of elm and white oak lead to groves of beech, maple, hawthorne, birch, honey locust, and Ohio buckeye. Fields of heather contrast with the varying greens of the junipers, firs, spruces, pines, and hemlocks. The flowering season begins in March with the first burst of the witch hazel and rhododendron, followed in April and May by Japanese cherry, dogwood, magnolia, flowering crab apple, white fringe tree, flowering quince, and golden chain tree. The summer flowering of the azaleas, Japanese snowbells, and Franklinia is followed by the brilliance of the fall foliage.

41

DESCANSO GARDENS

La Canada, California

Surrounded by the San Rafael hills, Descanso Gardens cover the last remaining acreage of the territory given to José Maria Verdugo by California Governor Pedro Fages in a Spanish land grant of 1784. During its long history as the famous Rancho San Rafael, prospectors discovered gold on the land and set up camp. Raided and pillaged by the notorious bandit, Lopez, they abandoned the venture. Some of the old stone foundations of the camp still remain. In the 1880's the land was again put to use, first as a cattle ranch and then as a vineyard. At the time Mr. Manchester Boddy discovered the property during weekend hiking trips with his sons, it was overgrown and undeveloped. Mr. Boddy, a Los Angeles newspaper publisher, purchased the one hundred sixty-five acres in the early 1930's. After building his home there, he immediately planted hundreds of camellias. Later he engaged the world famous rosarian, Dr. Walter Lammerts, to design a "History of the Rose Garden" and then a modern rose garden. Mr. Boddy opened his gardens to the public in 1951. Three years later the Los Angeles Board of Supervisors bought them, and under the direction of the Los Angeles Department of Arboreta and Botanic Gardens, expanded them. In co-operation with the public schools, nature-study programs are conducted. The former Boddy house is used as an educational center for workshops and lectures in horticulture and gardening.

Descanso, meaning "Where I Rest," has retained much that is nature-made. Fresh-water streams meander through woodlands of oaks, sycamores, ginkgos, and redwoods. The trails are banked by lilac, azalea, and rhododendron, which bloom in season. Thirty acres of native oak shade the more than one hundred thousand camellias. On the rim of the forest, the Sun Gardens of iris, native flora, and chrysanthemums are blended in color with the roses. The "History of the Rose Garden" has plantings of the leading varieties of roses from every period, beginning with the Christian Era, while the Modern Rose Garden is devoted to the All-American Rose Selections. An ever-increasing part of the cultural life of Los Angeles, Descanso is beautiful every month of the year.

43

SARAH P. DUKE GARDEN

Durham, North Carolina

The Duke Gardens are a memorial to the vision of Dr. Frederic M. Hanes, formerly of Duke Hospital, and the generosity of Mrs. Sarah P. Duke, widow of B. N. Duke, one of the founders of Duke University, and their daughter, Mrs. Mary Duke Biddle. In 1932, Dr. Hanes, an iris fancier, suggested that an iris garden be created in an untended valley on the university campus. With the financial support of Mrs. Duke, he engaged the noted horticulturalist John C. Wister to plan the garden of iris, spring bulbs, and flowering trees. In the spring of 1937, Mrs. Biddle donated a formal terraced garden, dedicated to the memory of her mother, "in whose life was blended the strength of the soil and the beauty of flowers." Ellen B. Shipman, a well-known landscape architect, designed the terraces. Later, a rock garden on the opposite slope was designed by Frederick H. Leubuscher. In 1947, the Department of Botany assumed the supervision of the gardens. Today, extensive plans are under way for further development and expansion.

On the upper slope a hedge of box, backed by a row of magnolias and a forest of pines, encloses the garden; hemlocks enclose the sides. Colorful beds of annuals and perennials, varied each year, bloom from early spring until autumn on each of the seven terraces of the formal garden. A wisteria-covered pergola overlooks the terraces which lead down to a water-lily pond. On the slope across the pond, evergreens, deciduous trees, and shrubs border the broad lawn. Thousands of narcissi cover the floor of the pine forest. Groups of flowering crab apples, cherries, peaches, forsythias, and quinces add a delicate touch to the garden in spring. In the fall—following the annuals, perennials, and numerous varieties of lilies that bloom throughout the summer—the greens of the pines, hollies, firethorns, and nandina contrast gaily with the changing foliage of the maples, sweet gums, and oaks.

DUMBARTON OAKS

Washington, D.C.

Dumbarton, the Georgian townhouse mansion of former Ambassador to Argentina, the Honorable Robert Woods Bliss, dates back to 1801. Widely traveled and with a deep interest in gardening, Mrs. Bliss consulted landscape architect Beatrix Farrand and created her formal country garden within the city. Mr. Bliss, a member of our diplomatic corps, served in many countries until his retirement in 1930. In 1940, Mr. and Mrs. Bliss gave Dumbarton Oaks, along with their library and collection of Byzantine and early Christian art, to the Trustees of Harvard University, who, each year, grant a Research Fellowship and two Resident Fellowships in landscape design. The house, now a museum, and the sixteen acres of gardens are open to the public.

46

Built on sharply sloping terrain, the garden is a series of terraces and winding paths leading through lawns into a woodland bordering on Rock Creek. Formal in design, the Beech Terrace, Urn Terrace, Fountain Terrace, and Rose Garden open onto a path edged with camellia, dogwood, and bamboo which leads to Lovers Lane Pool. The Pot Garden, with a teakwood pergola covered by wisteria, looks out over a vista of sloping lawn with beds of canterbury bell, foxglove, sweet william, alumroot, and phlox. A baroque shell fountain on a travertine pedestal separates the steps leading down to the swimming pool. Below the pool, the paths wind downhill through flowering crab and forsythia. In imaginative design, Dumbarton Oaks equals many of the estate gardens of Europe.

THE GARDENS OF THE GEORGE EASTMAN HOUSE

Rochester, New York

Throughout his life, George Eastman, the father of modern photography, had a thirst for flowers. His father, a nurseryman, died when George was six, leaving the family penniless. From then on George's one determination was to make enough money to provide for his mother and sisters. With his invention of the Kodak roll-film camera, he did this and more. In 1905, he built a

Georgian mansion for himself and his family and created a series of formal gardens and an arboretum on his ten-acre estate. His one domestic request was that flowers should always be displayed in the house. During his lifetime, George Eastman quietly, and often anonymously, gave away most of his private fortune. Upon his death in 1932, he left his house to the University of Rochester and for the next sixteen years it was used as the home of the president. In 1948, it was given to the George Eastman House, Inc., a nonprofit educational corporation, which, with a donation from the Eastman Kodak Company, turned the mansion into a Museum of Photography in memory of George Eastman.

The gardens have been restored to his original design. In the circular sunken garden, with a wisteria-covered pavilion created by Claude Bragdon and a Carl Milles sculpture-fountain, "Sunglitter," tulips abound in the spring and perennials throughout the summer months. In a long grass meadow enclosed by rare old trees with borders of tree peonies, the mirrorlike surface of

a pool reflects myriads of red roses. An herb garden and a cutting garden surround the neoclassic house which was George Eastman's birthplace in Waterville, N.Y., and which was moved to the museum grounds in 1954.

EDEN PARK CONSERVATORY

Cincinnati, Ohio

The display in the Eden Park Conservatory has been designed to show the relative beauty of the forms and textures of the plants rather than for scientific study. Built on a hillside in Eden Park, which takes its name from the Biblical garden, the conservatory is under the supervision of the Cincinnati Board of Park Commissioners. Since 1902, the Park Board had maintained propogation and show greenhouses on the site of the old Eden Park range. But over the years, as the show green-houses increased in popularity, two Park Commissioners, Irwin M. Krohn and Frederick Hinkle, persuaded the Board to build a conservatory solely for public enjoyment. It was completed in 1933.

Near the heart of Cincinnati, the conservatory overlooks the Ohio River. The permanent collections, in the Palm, Cacti, and Fern houses, include many rare specimens from the tropical climates of the world. In the Display House, seasonal floral exhibits continue throughout the year.

FAIRCHILD TROPICAL GARDEN

Coconut Grove, Florida

Inspired by David Fairchild's book, *Exploring for Plants*, Colonel Robert H. Montgomery, a New York tax attorney, decided to create a public botanical garden. In 1935, on the advice of his Florida neighbor, David Fairchild, famous plant explorer and scientist, he chose an eighty-three-acre tract on the limestone ridge between Miami and Cutler. William Lyman Phillips, a former associate of

Frederick Law Olmsted, designed the garden. On a visit to it, Dr. Harold Fletcher, Director of the Royal Botanic Garden in Edinburgh, described it as an excellent example of botanical-garden landscape design. Later, the Fairchild Tropical Garden Association turned over fifty-eight acres to the Park Department of Dade County, and the CCC built terraces, overlooks, and the pergola

52

for the Semple vine collection. The Park Department maintains this portion of the garden while the Association maintains the remaining twenty-five acres of the Montgomery Palmetum. The Montgomery Library, the Palm Products Museum, and the Nell Montgomery Auditorium, where lectures, workshops, and classes are held, form a part of the Palmetum. At the dedication ceremonies in 1938, the garden was named after David Fairchild. In 1940, the Garden Club of America awarded its Founder's Fund to the garden and in its honor an amphitheater was built for outdoor meetings. The broad paths of the garden lead through the individual groupings of vines, cycads, flowering tropical trees, and succulents. Its palm collection is the largest in the United States.

FORT WORTH BOTANIC GARDEN

Fort Worth, Texas

Rock Springs, where formerly Texas cowboys stopped to water their horses, is now a botanic garden. As Fort Worth expanded from a small cattle-trading town into a metropolis, the Park Board, in 1929, at the urging of the Garden Club, drew up plans for a garden. Later, with the aid of Federal Relief, WPA workmen spent three years constructing the eighty-five-acre garden. Four thousand tons of rock were hauled from Milsaps

to build terraces and walks and fill in swamps. Out of their meager pay, the workmen themselves raised seventy dollars to buy roses for the garden. In their honor, the Park Board has placed a plaque at the entrance. Since the garden's completion, a new rose area, a long maze modeled after one in the Hampton Court Gardens in London, and an arboretum with five hundred varieties of flowering fruit trees have been added. It is a demonstration garden for the All-American Rose Selections, and a test garden for the American Iris Society. The Garden Center houses the horticultural library and also serves as an educational center for ninety garden clubs.

The woodlands, formal and informal gardens, lakes and rolling lawns border on Trinity Park. In the herb garden, cactus garden, the annual and perennial gardens, rose gardens, iris garden, the holly and crape myrtle collections, along the nature trails, and in the lotus- and lily-covered waters of the lagoons, flowers bloom in their seasons. The procession which begins in late February with daffodils, camellias, azaleas, forsythia, and dogwood, is followed by roses, lotus, cacti, yucca, hibiscus, crape myrtle, annuals, dahlias, and chrysanthemums. Last of all come the bright-colored berries of the hollies, and nandinas, of native barberry and pyracantha. Elms, willows, cottonwoods, Spanish oaks, Indian wahoos, Chinese tallows, ashes, chinaberries, and persimmons shade the lawns of Bermuda grass.

on how to start garden clubs of their own. Today, Founders Memorial Garden is dedicated to the twelve ladies who started this first garden club.

The idea for the memorial garden originated in 1939 when Professor Hubert B. Owens, head of the Landscape Architecture Department of the University of Georgia, recommended to the Board of the Garden Club of Georgia that it be created in memory of the Ladies' Garden Club of Athens. With a donation from the Board, the Landscape Architecture Department designed the garden and began construction and planting in 1941. World War II interrupted their work, but in 1945, garden-club members and friends made contributions for a Living-Memorial Arboretum to be dedicated to garden club members' sons and daughters who had served in the war. At this time, too, the original garden was completed.

The garden serves as a laboratory for university students specializing in landscape design, horti-

FOUNDERS MEMORIAL GARDEN

Athens, Georgia

On a December morning in 1891, twelve ladies in Athens, Georgia, met and formed America's first organized garden club, The Ladies' Garden Club of Athens. They had no idea then that it would be the forerunner of thousands of garden clubs throughout the United States, and eventually of the Garden Club of America. At their first meeting, the ladies decided that "certain of its members would carry out experiments with different vegetables, flowers, and seeds to find out which varieties were best." On February 2, 1892, the Athens *Banner* mentioned that "The Ladies' Garden Club will accomplish much good if its members take a proper interest in it." They did take a "proper interest," and soon letters came from ladies in cities and towns throughout the nation asking for advice

56

culture, botany, and forestry. In 1951, the National Council of State Garden Clubs presented its coveted Silver Award to the Garden Club of Georgia in recognition of its work in creating this memorial. Again, in 1954, the National Council conferred its National Landscape Design Award on the Garden Club of Georgia.

Sitting on the edge of the university campus, the gardens surround the old Lumpkin House, originally built to house professors, but now the home of the Garden Club of Georgia. The former smokehouse has been converted into a memorial museum and trophy house. Blending in design with the Greek Revival architecture of the house and university itself, a formal boxwood garden with brick walks is enclosed by a white picket fence. On the terrace below, the perennial garden, with its broad lawn and pool, is enclosed by a serpentine walk. Tall pines and oaks shade the ground covers and azaleas in the adjoining garden. Ornamental trees and shrubs form a background for the seasonal bloom of the masses of camellias in the two informal gardens.

GARFIELD PARK
CONSERVATORY

Chicago, Illinois

One of the largest and most beautiful publicly owned gardens in the country, the conservatory is under the jurisdiction of the Chicago Park District, which maintains four hundred and nine parks in the Chicago area. Its four and a half acres is divided into seven main sections, ranging from the humid tropical world of palm, fern, and exotic blossom to the desert world of the American Southwest. In the Palm House, the cabbage palm, fanleaf palm, and the towering royal palm are set among bamboos and bananas. There are some one hundred eighty-five types of tropical trees and plants. The Fernery, once said by Lorado Taft to be "the most beautiful room in America," has an endless variety of graceful ferns covering rocks, climbing the rafters, and reflecting in pools. In the Airoid House, where the temperature never falls below 70 degrees, the emphasis is upon highly colored exotics—calathea, flamingo plant, episcia, and cordyline. The large forms of numerous philodendron contrast with the smaller forms of aerial vines. The naturalistic desert landscape of the Cactus House contains over four hundred varieties of cacti and succulents, including the rare senita, organ pipe, and saguaru. Coffee trees, fruit trees, herbs, and plants used in the manufacture of perfumes are among the one hundred ninety-two species of "useful plants" in the Economic House. The large Horticultural Hall has constantly changing flower shows throughout the seasons, including the azalea and camellia show in the spring, the begonia and caladium show in the summer, the chrysanthemum show in the fall, ending with the flaming red, pink, and white poinsettia show at Christmas.

GOLDEN GATE PARK
CONSERVATORY

San Francisco,
California

The "old-lace" Victorian Conservatory in Golden Gate Park is a replica of the conservatory in Kew Gardens, England. In the early 1870's, James Lick, a San Francisco philanthropist, commissioned the firm of Lord and Burnham at Irvington-on-the-Hudson, New York, to build a conservatory for his estate in San Jose, California. The structure, plus thirty-three tons of glass, was shipped from Irvington in a chartered sailing vessel, by way of Cape Horn. Before it was assembled, Mr. Lick died. He left the unopened boxes of glass to the Society of California Pioneers, who, in turn, sold it to the City of San Francisco. In 1887, the building was assembled in Golden Gate on Plateau Mound, later renamed Mount Lick.

Standing sedately atop a sloping terrace on the Park's main drive the Conservatory covers fifteen thousand square feet of ground. In its warm and humid atmosphere one of the most notable collections of tropical plants in the United States has been developed. In the Palm House some of the oldest and largest philodendron plants in cultivation surround the rare palms. Tropical water lilies, in the raised pool of the Fern House, add color to the varying greens of the lacy ferns. Bougainvillea, large-flowered hibiscus, and orchids blend with the brilliant foliage of the crotons in the Croton House. The seasonal display of flowering plants in the Cool House begins in January with cyclamen, followed by cinerarias, lilies, calceolarias, schizanthus, tuberous begonias, and chrysanthemums, ending in December with Christmas poinsettias.

THE HERSHEY GARDENS

Hershey, Pennsylvania

Milton S. Hershey, founder of the candy firm and of the town of Hershey, Pennsylvania, once said, "The more beautiful the community, the happier the people." When he started his first chocolate plant in 1903, he envisioned building a town with gardens, parks, playgrounds, and community centers. Eventually his dream came true, and in 1936, under his supervision, the Hershey Gardens were created. Originally the three-and-a-half-acre plot was solely a rose garden. It was opened to the

62

public in 1937. At the American Rose Society's dedication of the garden in 1938, Dr. J. Horace McFarland, one of the organizers of the Society, said, "These are roses shown at their best. It is a garden education; a real university of rose lore gathered and nurtured into beauty." In 1941, Mr. Hershey purchased an additional seventeen acres of farmland adjoining the gardens. Here he planted trees, shrubs, and evergreens around beds of annuals and perennials. Today, the gardens reflect Mr. Hershey's original idea of beauty for the sole benefit of the people.

Perched on a hillside overlooking the Lebanon Valley, the gardens offer an array of color from March through November. The terraces are dazzling with roses—climbers, hybrid teas, rugosas, perpetuals, and polyanthas, as well as special blooms—from May until October. In early spring, narcissi, hyacinths, crocuses, and anemones are followed by a magnificent display of tulips.

Throughout the summer, beds of annuals and perennials cover the sloping lawns, followed in early autumn by a chrysanthemum display. In their season, from March until October, azaleas, redbud, mock orange, pink and white dogwood, weigela, quince, jasmine, and rhododendron add color. Background plantings of California redwoods, spruces, firs, junipers, and hemlocks surround the garden, while beeches, poplars, maples, locusts, birches, and oaks shade the lawns.

HIGHLAND AND DURAND — EASTMAN PARK ARBORETUM

Rochester, New York

The six hundred acres in these two parks comprise one of the largest and finest arboretums in the United States. In 1887, George Ellwanger and William Barry, owners of one of the largest nurseries in their time, gave the city twenty acres of rolling wooded hills which had been shaped thousands of years ago by a stalled glacier. A year later, Frederick Law Olmsted was called in by the Park Commission to design Highland Park and draw up plans for future parks. Mr. Ellwanger and Mr. Barry gave specimens from their nursery for the first planting. Later trees and shrubs from other American nurseries were added. Before quarantine curtailed the free flow of plants from abroad, the park had imported a collection that would be impossible to duplicate today. The second oldest arboretum in the country, Highland Park today has over fourteen hundred species of trees and shrubs. Its famous lilac collection includes many varieties which originated at the park. In 1908, two of Rochester's leading citizens, Dr. Henry Durand and George Eastman, gave the city four hundred eighty-four acres bordering on Lake Ontario. This park was planted with grasses and vegetation to stabilize erosion. Two small lakes were built, and evergreens, flowering trees, and shrubs were planted. Today the park has an excellent collection of conifers as well as malus, magnolia, and prunus.

HODGES GARDENS

Many, Louisiana

Hodges Garden, Experimental Area, and Game and Wildlife Refuge is dedicated to the conservation and creation of beauty. When A. J. Hodges Industries purchased forty-three hundred acres in a belt composed equally of longleaf and shortleaf pine, the trees were being starved out by worth-

less scrub oak. To improve the native pines, a program of hybridization and selective cutting was immediately started. This experimental work was carried on with the advice of two specialists, Dr. Philip Wakely of the Southern Forest Experiment Station and Dr. Bruce Zobel of the Texas Forest

Service. As it progressed, the natural beauty of the area inspired the idea of a "garden in the forest." In 1952, three hundred acres were set aside for the garden and the wildlife refuge. An old rock quarry was chosen as the site of the garden, and its natural features formed the design. The former tram tracks were replaced with walks, waterfalls were constructed in eroded areas, a pool was built in an old swimming hole, and trees which had started from wind-blown seeds were left to grow among mounds of broken rock. The garden was opened to the public in 1959.

Throughout this man-and-nature-made garden there is a blend of flowers, rocks, trees, and water. In the bottom of the quarry, the paths wind along streams, through rock mounds, and over pine-needle floors splashed with beds of seasonal blossoming flowers. On the hillside above the lake, a wisteria-covered pavilion looks out over the rose garden with some two thousand bushes of many varieties blooming from March through November. In the greenhouses, the blossoms of delicate flowers and vines sparkle colorfully against the green-hued tropical foliage plants.

HOYT
ARBORETUM

Portland, Oregon

Hoyt Arboretum sits on a gently sloping hill surrounded by the Cascade Mountains and the Columbia and Willamette rivers. During National Forestry Week in 1928, a committee of tree-lovers headed by Thornton T. Munger of the U. S. Forest Service proposed to the City Council, ". . . since the city is now one of the largest centers of the lumbering industry of the Northwest, a muncipal arboretum should be established to preserve the various species of conifers for the benefit of future generations." The resolution was adopted, the county set aside two hundred thirteen acres, and the first trees were planted in 1931. Many of them have been kept in their natural habitats and very few nurserymen's varieties have been added. Nearly all the plant material used at the arboretum is supplied by the Park Bureau's Mt. Tabor Nursery and the U. S. Forest Service's experiment station at Wind River. The arboretum is constantly used by garden clubs and nature-study groups for the identification of exotic as well as native species of trees.

The temperate climate and bountiful rainfall of the region is well suited for the culture of conifers. Today the arboretum has one of the largest and finest collections of fir, cedar, larch, juniper, pine, spruce, yew, hemlock, California nutmeg, and Japanese cryptomeria in the country. Throughout the grounds native ferns and wild flowers nestle in the grass, at the foot of the trees, along the trails, and on the banks of the streams.

A Young Birch

The birch begins to crack its outer sheath
Of baby green and show the white beneath,
As whosoever likes the young and slight
May well have noticed. Soon entirely white
To double day and cut in half the dark
It will stand forth, entirely white in bark,
And nothing but the top a leafy green—
The only native tree that dares to lean,
Relying on its beauty, to the air.
(Less brave perhaps than trusting are the fair.)
And someone reminiscent will recall
How once in cutting brush along the wall
He spared it from the number of the slain,
At first to be no bigger than a cane,
And then no bigger than a fishing pole,
But now at last so obvious a bole
The most efficient help you ever hired
Would know that it was there to be admired,
And zeal would not be thanked that cut it down
When you were reading books or out of town.
It was a thing of beauty and was sent
To live its life out as an ornament.

Founders Memorial Garden, *Athens, Georgia*

Winterthur, *Wilmington, Delaware*

Longwood Gardens, *Kennett Square, Pennsylvania*

Airlie Gardens, *Wilmington, North Carolina*

Kingwood Center, *Mansfield, Ohio*

The Morris Arboretum, *Chestnut Hill, Pennsylvania*

Rose Pogonias

A saturated meadow,
  Sun-shaped and jewel-small,
A circle scarcely wider
  Than the trees around were tall;
Where winds were quite excluded,
  And the air was stifling sweet,
With the breath of many flowers,—
  A temple of the heat.

There we bowed us in the burning,
  As the sun's right worship is,
To pick where none could miss them
  A thousand orchises;
For though the grass was scattered,
  Yet every second spear
Seemed tipped with wings of color,
  That tinged the atmosphere.

We raised a simple prayer
  Before we left the spot,
That in the general mowing
  That place might be forgot;
Or if not all so favored,
  Obtain such grace of hours,
That none should mow the grass there
  While so confused with flowers.

WALTER HUNNEWELL ARBORETUM
Wellesley, Massachusetts

Three generations of the Hunnewell family have dedicated themselves to the development of one of the finest arboretums in the United States. Horatio Hollis Hunnewell, a Boston banker and founder of the arboretum, showed an interest in horticulture at an early age. He relates in his diary: "When a dozen years old, I planted some cherry-stones in my father's garden which came up and I budded them. These trees my father sold and sent me over fifty dollars as the proceeds. So the first money I ever earned was in the nursery business." In 1846, Mr. Hunnewell started the arboretum on twenty acres with evergreen, fruit, and forest trees imported from England. By 1852, he had added one hundred seventeen acres to the arboretum and had introduced azaleas and imported rhododendrons. Until his death in 1902, Mr. Hunnewell personally supervised the development of the area. When Walter Hunnewell inherited the arboretum from his father, he reduced it to forty acres and stressed the planting and study of trees and shrubs hardy to the New England climate. Since his death in 1921, his son, Walter Hunnewell, Jr., the present owner, has added many new plants and has kept the arboretum open to the public.

Situated at the edge of Lake Waban, the arboretum adjoins the campus of Wellesley College. On the hillside above the lake, the clipped trees in "the oldest topiary in America" are patterned after the trees in Italian gardens of the middle 1800's. In the Pinetum, spruces, hemlocks, yews, cedars, firs, oaks, beeches, elms, and junipers cover the hillsides and surround the broad lawns. The rhododendrons represent the finest collection in New England.

HENRY E.
HUNTINGTON
LIBRARY
GARDENS

San Marino, California

The Henry E. Huntington Gardens, Library, and Art Galleries offer one of the richest collections of plants, manuscripts, and art works in America. A businessman and philanthropist, Mr. Huntington accumulated a fortune from the development of real estate in southern California. On his two-hundred-acre estate he built a Georgian mansion in 1910 and began to fill it with his rare collection of art. After ten years, he built the library to house the overflow. He personally supervised the development of his gardens. In 1919, Mr. Huntington deeded the estate as a free research library, art gallery, and botanical garden for the benefit of the public. Today, the seven principal art galleries and fifteen smaller ones house over four hundred art objects, and the Library contains approximately two hundred thousand rare books, letters, and documents.

The two-hundred-acre botanical garden, containing over fifty thousand plants, is distinguished for its variety and for its tasteful landscaping. The desert garden has the largest outdoor group of cacti and other succulents in the world. In the Italian style, the rose garden is centered around a long colonnaded pergola. The five-acre camellia garden, containing over a thousand varieties, is a test garden for the American Camellia Society. A small canyon has been transformed into a traditional Japanese garden with a moon bridge spanning a stream, a rock garden, and flowering trees. Throughout the estate there are magnificent sweeps of park and lawn, with fountains and sculpture binding the individual garden into a harmony of landscape.

Nestled in the West Side Hills, overlooking the "City of Roses," the garden was started in the early days of World War I by three of America's leading nurserymen, E. G. Hill of Indiana, Robert Pyle of Pennsylvania, and George Morris of Ohio. Here they were fortunate in finding suitable soil and climate, as well as the help of Jesse A. Curry, an ardent rosarian and then a regional trustee of the American Rose Society. In 1917, the City of Portland's Park Bureau took over the development and maintenance, and a few years later, details and measurements of the roses were sent for evaluation to Dean Hole, President of the National Rose Society of England. He wrote, "Portland

THE INTERNATIONAL ROSE
TEST GARDEN

Portland, Oregon

roses are equal to any of the prize beauties in England." In addition to serving as a testing ground for the American Rose Society and the All-American Rose Selections, the garden also tests roses from many foreign countries.

The garden, which grows every known type of rose, is on a slope in Washington Park with three broad terraces and nine separate rose areas. Flanked by flowering plums, the Rosarian Garden with formal beds honors Jesse Curry. Thousands of varieties bloom in the display gardens, among them, Sonata, Juno, Tiffany, Rubaiyat, and Masquerade, which are among former winners of the "City of Portland's Gold Medal" represented in the Gold Medal Award Garden. Queen Elizabeth is the only rose in the Shakespearian Garden of boxwood-edged beds of annuals and perennials.

76

JAPANESE HOUSE AND GARDEN

West Fairmont Park, Philadelphia, Pennsylvania

The Buddhist monks who introduced the land-scape garden to Japan expressed in their designs the mood of nature and the mood of man. A garden was planned in relationship to the occupation of its owner, whether warrior or poet. The house in West Fairmont Park, designed by the noted architect Junzo Yoshimura, and the garden, designed by landscape architect Tansai Sano, are based on a sixteenth- or seventeenth-century home for a man with leisure for contemplation. In 1955, the house was presented to the people of the United States by the American-Japan Society on behalf of the people of Japan. Its design was chosen to show the Japanese influence on modern Western architecture. Built in Nagoya, the house was sent to this country and reassembled in the garden of the Museum of Modern Art. In 1957, the Museum presented it to the City of Philadelphia.

In the Japanese tradition, the garden symbolizes the world and the spirit. The stream with water plants and flowers, beneath the bridge leading to the teahouse, runs into a larger stream which represents the river; the river flows into the lotus pond which signifies the ocean. Dwarf bamboo and pine represent a forest, and a waterfall in the forest empties into the ocean. Rocks from Nagoya, pointing toward heaven, suggest a temple; others, protruding from the water, the islands of Japan.

KINGWOOD CENTER

Mansfield, Ohio

Kingwood is a lively cultural center as well as a garden for the people of Mansfield. Charles Kelley King, for many years head of the Ohio Brass Company, in 1953, left his endowed estate to the people of his community. With a keen interest in horticulture and nature study acquired from a Maine boyhood, Mr. King developed the formal gardens

80

and greenhouses on his forty-seven-acres. King Hall, a large Norman mansion and his former home, now houses the horticultural library and is a center for flower shows, art shows, lectures, and concerts. Research at the center is devoted to the development and study of native plants and to test gardens for the American Daffodil Society, the American Peony Society, the All-American Chrysanthemum Selections, and the American Hemerocallis Society.

Lying at the west edge of town, Kingwood, with its rolling lawns, formal gardens, greenhouses, and woodlands, has blooms throughout the seasons. In spring the flowering of the eranthis, scillas and crocuses is followed by the daffodils and hyacinths. The spectacular display of tulips comes at the end of April. The roses start their six months of bloom in June, along with the iris and peonies. The flowering of the lilies, annuals, gladioli, and perennials spread throughout the summer months. When summer wanes, the bloom of the dahlias is followed by the turn of the foliage and the chrysanthemum display. Winding through a forest of maple, elm, pine and hickory, dogwood and beech, the Nature Trail is alive with bobwhite quail and chukar partridges roaming among Solomon's seal and prairie rose, meadowsweet and jack-in-the-pulpit, wild geranium and nodding trillium, lily of the valley and flowering raspberry, wintergreen, bluebells, asters, and ferns. Kingwood is a showplace for gardeners and for all interested in nature and bird study.

81

THE KITCHEN GARDEN
OF MOUNT VERNON

Mount Vernon, Virginia

George Washington once wrote to a friend, "It is true that to be a cultivator of Land has been my favorite amusement." Soon after Washington took possession of Mt. Vernon upon the death of his brother, Lawrence, in 1752, he left to become Commander of the Virginia Militia. In 1758, he returned to settle at Mt. Vernon and a year later married Martha Dandridge Custis. Keenly interested in the development of the property surrounding his county seat, he ordered Batty Langley's *New Principles of Gardening* from his London agent. In 1760, he designed the Kitchen Garden and, eight years later, the Flower Garden. Through the succeeding years he imported gardeners from England, Holland, Scotland, and Germany. In his diary he mentions one of these gardeners, "Mr. Wilming, the German Gentleman offered to engage a gardener for me and to send him in a ship from Bremen . . . he is to be a compleat Kitchen Gardener with a competent knowledge of Flowers and a Greenhouse." When General Washington returned to Mt. Vernon after the Revolution, he had the gardens reconstructed by Samuel Vaughan. After Washington's death in 1799, the area was used solely for growing foodstuffs and the design of the garden disappeared. In 1936, with the aid of garden books in Washington's library, his diaries, and his gardener's weekly reports, the Mount

Vernon Ladies' Association restored the Kitchen Garden to its original design.

With traditional eighteenth-century balance and symmetry, the garden is a combination of beauty and usefulness. Espaliered fruit trees form patterns along the brick walls; others form cordons along the brick and turf paths separating the herb-bordered beds. Throughout the garden there are sixty different varieties of herbs and vegetables, including lemon balm, hyssop, germander, thyme, basil, anise, rosemary, lavender, rhubarb, broccoli, carrots, cabbages, peppers, artichokes, and turnips. The dipping cistern, open to the light and air for softening, serves for watering the plants, and the beehives provide a table sweet and candle wax.

83

THE GARDENS OF LONGFELLOW HOUSE

Portland, Maine

The gardens about which Henry Wadsworth Long-fellow often wrote have been in existence since 1785. When his grandfather, Major General Peleg Wadsworth, moved from Duxbury, Massachusetts, to Portland, Maine, to take over the coastal command during the Revolution, he bought an acre and a half of land, built a brick colonial house, and planted fruit trees. Mrs. Wadsworth added herbs, marigolds, and crimson Boursalt roses which she had brought from her garden in Duxbury. After the war, General Wadsworth moved to Hiram, Maine, leaving his house in Portland to his daugh-

ter, Zilpah, the mother of Henry Wadsworth Longfellow. Here the poet resided until he left for Europe in 1826, but throughout his life, he often returned to visit his sister, Anne Longfellow Pierce. Upon her death in 1910, she left the house, now a museum, to the Maine Historical Society. In 1924, the garden was restored by the Longfellow Garden Club.

The long narrow garden is enclosed by a brick wall covered with Virginia creeper, China fleece vine, and Chinese wisteria. Ground covers and beds of annuals and perennials are shaded by hawthorn, mountain ash, and mulberry. Longfellow wrote of the garden, "The lilacs are in bloom and the apple trees. The whole world is a flower garden; and the birds are singing, singing, singing!"

LONGWOOD GARDENS

Kennett Square, Pennsylvania

Created for "the enjoyment of all," Longwood abundantly fulfills its purpose. It was on a Sunday afternoon drive through the rolling countryside of southeastern Pennsylvania, in 1906, that Pierre du Pont noticed cutting marks on many of the trees in "Pierce Park." Collected from far and wide, these hundred-year-old trees had been planted by the Pierce brothers in this "long-wooded" grove on a tract granted to their family by William Penn in 1702. To save the arboretum, Pierre du Pont bought the thousand-acre tract, where, during the Revolution, one of the first skirmishes of the Battle of Brandywine had been fought. Calling it Longwood, he established his country estate there

86

and personally supervised the development of the gardens. Longwood is lavish in variety. With formal gardens, small flowering gardens, yew and rose gardens, an arboretum, natural lakes and pools, and conservatories and hothouses, it is many gardens in one. In the Georgian-designed conservatories there is a year-round, ever-changing display of bloom. The hothouses are the largest in the world. The water garden, with blue-tiled pools bordered with ivy and enclosed by juniper hedges, is patterned after a garden at the Villa Gamberaia near Florence. Famous for its outdoor formal garden, where by day fountains spray in translucent coolness and by night geyser in an array of colors, Longwood has been compared to the gardens of Versailles in France, the Borghesi in Italy, and Hampstead Heath in England.

LOS ANGELES STATE
AND COUNTY ARBORETUM

Arcadia, California

Until the late 1840's, the site of the Los Angeles State and County Arboretum was a mission rancho. Deeded to an Indian woman, Dona Victoria, for her services as a housekeeper for the padres of the San Gabriel Mission, the property was first developed by her husband, Hugo Reid. Following the Reids, a succession of owners worked the land, leaving their own legacy in trees, buildings, and nostalgic atmosphere. Of all of these, none was more colorful than "Lucky" Baldwin who shared in the profits from the Comstock Lode. He spent a fortune in developing the rancho to its highest peak of productivity. A lavish host, he built the "Queen Anne Cottage" with gingerbread trim, tower, and period gardens, all of which have been restored at the arboretum. After Baldwin's death in 1909, the property was deserted. In 1947, at the instigation of the Southern California Horticultural Institute, the State of California and the County of Los Angeles jointly purchased one hundred twenty-seven acres of the old rancho. The arboretum, which has a varied educational and research program, is administered by the County in co-operation with the California Arboretum Foundation.

Four major areas in the arboretum are devoted to plantings of those countries of the world having a climate similar to that of Southern California. The Australian collection includes more than three hundred species and varieties of eucalyptus and two hundred species of acacia. The aloe group is outstanding in the South African collection, and in the jungle area there is a representative collection of palms as well as over sixty varieties of bamboo. The Oriental collection includes plants from every part of the Far East. The herb garden is one of the largest in the country. A demonstration garden with plants in landscaped settings is a guide for homeowners interested in creating their own small gardens.

MAGNOLIA GARDENS

Charleston, South Carolina

After a visit to Magnolia Gardens, the late British novelist, John Galsworthy, wrote, "Nothing so free and gracious, so lovely and richly colored, exists, planted by man." From the beginning, when Thomas Drayton, of English descent, emigrated in 1671 from Barbados and settled at Magnolia-on-the-Ashley, the plantation was one of great natural beauty. Noted for Magnolia grandiflora, from which it took its name, Magnolia had one of the most stately mansions in all of Carolina. Destroyed

by fire shortly after the Revolution, this house was replaced by one of cypress, which also was burned during the Civil War. Now Norwood Hastie, a ninth-generation descendant of Thomas Drayton, occupies the third house. The present gardens were planned and developed by the Reverend John Grimke-Drayton whose grandfather, Thomas Drayton II, willed the plantation to him on condition that he take the name Drayton. Rev. Drayton imported the first plantings of Camellia japonica to Magnolia in 1843, and five years later, the first plantings of Azalea indica. After an illness in 1851, Rev. Drayton, on the advice of his physician, "took to the soil to dig." His first plantings were one red rose and one white rose at the foot of the ivy-covered steps of his house. Soon after the Civil War he opened Magnolia Gardens to the public.

Bordered on one side by shimmering loblollies, tree magnolias, and cedars, and on the other by the easy flow of the tidal waters of the Ashley, Magnolia is "other worldly." Its collection of Camellia japonica and Azalea indica is one of the finest in the country. With the shifting of the sun's rays through the ancient moss-covered trees casting light and shadow among the clusters of bloom, Magnolia is a garden of mystery and enchantment.

MIDDLETON GARDENS

Charleston, South Carolina

For more than two centuries, Middleton Gardens have been as famous as the distinguished family who created them. In 1741, Henry Middleton, President of the First Continental Congress, drew up the original design, based on Le Notre's gardens at Versailles. His son, Arthur, a signer of the Dec-

laration of Independence, engaged French botanist André Michaux to bring the first Camellia japonica to the United States. Arthur's son, Henry, a former governor of South Carolina, imported masses of camellias, and when Williams Middleton inherited the plantation in 1846, he added hundreds of azaleas. During the Civil War, the mansion was almost totally destroyed, but today the south wing has been restored by the present owner, J. J. Pringle Smith, a descendant of Henry Middleton. In 1941, the Garden Club of America awarded Middleton its coveted Bulkley Medal for "200 years of enduring beauty."

Overlooking the Ashley River, a broad lawn slopes down to Butterfly Lake. On the hillsides surrounding the plantation's old rice mill, masses of azaleas blaze in brilliance beneath moss-covered branches of live oak. Pools reflect towering magnolias and the pink and lavender of the azaleas. From the axis of Sundial Circle, paths fan out to the nine-hundred-year-old Middleton Oak, to the largest camellia planting in the country, and to allées of camellias.

MISSOURI BOTANICAL GARDEN

"Shaw's Garden," St. Louis, Missouri

When Henry Shaw came to St. Louis from Shef-
field, England, he often spent his Sundays riding
out into the country on horseback to observe the
changes in the colors of nature. An enterprising
young merchant, he invested in his own idea of
shipping New Orleans sugar up the Mississippi
River to St. Louis rather than by land. After making a fortune in his venture, he retired into the
same countryside he had known as a young man.
In 1849, he built a large rambling house, and with
the aid of his friend, Sir Joseph Hooker, Director
of the Royal Botanic Gardens at Kew, England,
began to plant the grounds. Ten years later, he
built a library and herbarium and sent his friend,
Dr. George Engelmann, prominent surgeon and
botanist, to Europe to buy botanical books and
herbarium specimens. He hired a curator for the

library and herbarium and brought Mr. James
Guerney from England to supervise the garden.
In 1859, he opened it to the public and named it
the Missouri Botanical Garden. For the next thirty
years, Mr. Shaw personally directed the garden.
When he died, in 1889, the place was internation-
ally famous. In keeping with Mr. Shaw's tradition
of maintaining a great botanical garden, the Climatron, the only geodesic-dome greenhouse in the
world, was constructed. Based on an R. Buck-
minister Fuller design, it was opened to the public
in 1960.

In the Climatron, tropical and semitropical
plants have a natural setting. Outside, the night-
and day-blooming tropical hybrid water lilies that
cover the pools originated at the garden. From
late January until Christmas, there are displays of
colorful bloom.

95

THE GARDEN OF THE MOFFATT-LADD HOUSE

Portsmouth, New Hampshire

The colonial mansion on Market Street was built in 1764 for Samuel Moffatt and his bride by Samuel's father, John Moffatt, one of the earliest settlers in Portsmouth. The house was the center of social activity in the town until Samuel Moffatt, whose "college education and fashionable life had not qualified him for strict and prudent application in business," became heavily in debt. To escape imprisonment he secretly sailed to the West Indies. John Moffatt repurchased the house and lived in it with his daughter, Catherine. When William Whipple, a signer of the Declaration of Independence, married Catherine Moffatt, he moved into his father-in-law's house. The Whipples were childless and upon their death, a town physician, Dr. Havan, bought the estate for his daughter and son-in-law, Alexander Ladd. When their son, Alexander Hamilton Ladd, inherited the property in 1862, he devoted much of his time and energy to the development of the garden. He planted the magnificent wisteria which today curtains the western wall of the house, built the turf steps leading to the rose arbor, and laid out the lawn and curved paths in the garden. Many of the bulbs that he imported from Holland still survive. He wrote in his garden book an expression of thanks to his Lord for giving him the happiness of living out his life "in so sweet and retired a spot of this beautiful world." After his death in 1900, the estate was neglected until 1913, when the Colonial Dames of New Hampshire leased it and restored both house and garden.

A dense wall of shrubbery, planted against a paneled fence, surrounds the garden, secluding it from the life of the city. The paths lead over tree-shaded lawns, past an old bee skep, through the grape arbor, and up terraces splashed with turf-banked flower beds, to the original herb garden. A sundial, which once told the time in the garden of the Earl of Ranfurley, County Tyrone, Ireland, is centered on one terrace. A flight of soft-green turfed steps leads up through a long allée of arbors covered with pink and white roses.

THE MORRIS ARBORETUM

Chestnut Hill, Pennsylvania

The arboretum, which now has one of the finest collections of trees and shrubs in the United States, was created by John T. Morris and his sister, Lydia Morris, in 1887, on eighty-five acres surrounding their former summer home, "Compton." During their travels throughout the world, the Morrises collected seeds, plants, and trees, and through their generous support of numerous expeditions, including those sponsored by the Arnold Arboretum of Harvard University, they acquired

plants from southeastern Asia. With the exception of the Japanese gardens, John Morris personally planned the arboretum. After his death in 1915, Miss Morris continued it in the tradition of her brother, adding a Rose Garden and a Rock Wall Garden. Upon her death in 1932, she left the arboretum to the University of Pennsylvania, together with funds for continuing the work. The university has increased the size of the arboretum to one hundred seventy acres. In 1948, it purchased the adjoining estate, "Overlea," which, renamed "Thomas Sovereign Gates Hall," houses the library, the herbarium, and the research laboratories.

Throughout the arboretum there are trees and shrubs from Europe and Asia, as well as eastern North America, among them fine collections of ivy, holly, and boxwood. As recipient of the winners of the American Rose Society's annual awards, the arboretum's rose garden displays the finest varieties. With the Founders' Fund Award of the Garden Club of America, the arboretum has recently added a medicinal-plant garden.

MORTON ARBORETUM

Lisle, Illinois

After his first visit to the Arnold Arboretum in Boston, at the age of nineteen, Joy Morton told his father that someday he would like to found a similar one in the Middle West. His interest came naturally. J. Sterling Morton, his father, was an avid conservationist, the originator of Arbor Day

and Secretary of Agriculture under President Grover Cleveland. In 1917, with Charles Sprague Sargent, Director of the Arnold Arboretum, and O. C. Simonds, Chicago landscape architect, Joy Morton worked out a plan for an arboretum on the grounds of his house, "Thornhill." Five years later, he added another seven hundred twenty-five acres. During the following eleven years, nearly four hundred thousand trees and shrubs were planted and the arboretum was expanded to thirteen hundred twenty-five acres. Today, the arboretum has an extensive educational program.

Set among rolling hills, natural forest, ponds, and lakes, the arboretum has arranged its plantings according to botanical, geographical, and landscape groups. The Evergeen, Thornhill, and Forest Nature trails wind through massive tree collections. In June and July, the old-fashioned rose garden adds brilliance to the greens of the formal and informal hedge demonstration plantings.

101

THE MOUNTAIN LAKE
SANCTUARY

Lake Wales, Florida

Mountain Lake is a Netherlander's tribute to America. In 1863, at the age of six, Edward William Bok immigrated to the United States from Den Helder. Years later, he became editor of *The Ladies' Home Journal* and won a Pulitzer Prize for his autobiography, *The Americanization of Edward Bok*. When he retired in 1919 and bought an estate at Mountain Lake, Florida, he remembered the saying of his grandmother, "Make you the world a bit better or more beautiful because you have lived in it," and decided to turn his home into a sanctuary for people who love beauty and quiet. The eighty acres of pine-clad hillside were soon transformed into a garden by renowned landscape architect Frederic Law Olmsted. Inspired by the bell tower at Malines, Belgium,

Milton B. Medary designed a Singing Tower for the sanctuary. In 1929, Calvin Coolidge, then President of the United States, dedicated the Mountain Lake Sanctuary, which has since served, as Bok said, "to preach the gospel of beauty."

The sixty-eight-acre garden sits atop Iron Mountain, the highest point in Florida. Live oaks, long-leaf pines, palms, laurel cherries, yaupons, and palmettos enclose Bermuda and rye-grass lawns banked by azaleas, lilies, oleanders, and camellias. Crape myrtle, jasmine, and viburnum add fragrance to the garden. Ferns cover the banks of the tree-shaded lakes and pools where black and white swans float serenely, and hundreds of birds find protection among the trees and shrubbery.

MUIR WOODS

Mill Valley,

California

Muir Woods National Monument preserves a virgin stand of native redwood in a four-hundred-eighty-five-acre forest just north of San Francisco. The area was the gift of U. S. Congressman William Kent and his wife, Elizabeth Thacher Kent, in 1908, and was established by presidential proclamation as a part of our National Park System. At the request of the donors, the woods were named in honor of John Muir, naturalist, writer, and one of the foremost advocates of our national parks. He spent most of his life in the exploration and study of the wild beauty of the West, and the stately grandeur of the forest is a fitting memorial to him. The trails wind through the heart of the forest and are shaded from the sun by Douglas firs, red alders, California buckeyes, tanbark oaks, California bay, and towering coastal redwoods, some over eighteen hundred years old. A profusion of lacy ferns and velvety mosses cover the tree bases, fallen vegetation, and the rocks along the banks of Redwood Creek. Clumps of trillium, adder's-tongue, and clintonia are scattered over the forest floor. Bobcats, deer, and racoons make an occasional visit to the forest. With the coming of spring, Western azaleas reflect their blossoms in the stream where salmon fingerlings swim up from the Pacific to spawn.

THE GARDEN OF THE
MUSEUM OF MODERN ART

New York, New York

At its opening in 1929, the Museum of Modern Art was one of the first museums in the country to exhibit the paintings of the then relatively unknown painters Cézanne, Van Gogh, Gauguin, and Seurat. In this same tradition, it was the first museum in America to create a garden for the exhibition of modern sculpture. The garden, opened in 1953, was designed by Philip Johnson, Director of the Museum's Department of Architecture and Design, and named after one of the Museum's founders, Abbey Aldrich Rockefeller.

The sunken garden, in the shadow of the towers of Manhattan skyscrapers, is paved with gray Vermont marble. It is enclosed on the west by a terrace banked with creeping roses and winter jasmine protected by European hornbeams. On the north, plane trees, Hankow willows, and a small Japanese styrax frame the gray brick wall. On the east, ailanthus, gray birch, rhododendrons, azaleas, grape hyacinths, and Geneva bugle curtain the garden from city buildings. On the south, weeping beeches, draping over a ground cover of lily of the valley, reflect in the glass walls of the museum itself. Two reflecting pools and a grove of Japanese cedars, greenbriers, and honeysuckle divide the garden into areas for the exhibition of the permanent collection of sculpture by Matisse, Rodin, Maillol, Lachaise, Moore, and Lipchitz. Beneath a grove of European birches, beds of bright flowers add seasonal color.

NATIONAL ARBORETUM

Washington, D.C.

Sitting on the edge of the nation's capital, the National Arboretum is the only federally sponsored arboretum in the country. It was established in 1927 by an Act of Congress and is administered by the Secretary of Agriculture through the Crop Research Division of the Agricultural Research Service. The Secretary is assisted in the development of the arboretum by an advisory committee of citizens and representatives of interested organizations. With an intermediate climate, the arboretum is able to cultivate plants from many countries, and its aim is to stimulate the interest of the

public in these unusual plants. As a research center, it maintains an herbarium of thousands of plant specimens and sponsors projects in plant naming and in the breeding and testing of new varieties of woody plants. It is a test garden for the American Peony Society, and its holly collection is grown in co-operation with the Holly Society of America. The plantings in the Cryptomeria Valley, Cedrus Valley, and Himalayan Pine Valley were made possible through donations by the Garden Club of America; the National Farm and Garden Association contributed dogwoods; and the National Capital Garden Club sponsored Fern Valley.

The arboretum covers four hundred seventeen acres of meadows, stream-edged woodlands, fields, and lakes. The display of azaleas on Morrison Hill is the most extensive in the United States. Natural woodlands form a background for pears, magnolias, Japanese quinces, rhododendrons, flowering cherries, crab apples, dogwoods, camellias, peonies, and crape myrtle, as well as for the collections of maple, beech, redwood, birch, cedar, black walnut, cypress, and of white, Spanish, and willow oak, which blend into the natural landscape.

"NAUMKEAG GARDENS"

The Choate Estate, Stockbridge, Massachusetts

With a mid-Victorian air, Naumkeag represents an era that is quietly fading. Left by Mabel Choate to the Trustees of Reservations upon her death in 1958, Naumkeag was her family's summer home. The name originates from the Indian word for Salem, the birthplace of Miss Choate's father, Joseph H. Choate, a prominent lawyer and Ambassador to the Court of St. James's. In 1885, Stanford White designed the house and Nathaniel Barrett planned the original gardens to the north. The Linden Walk was added after Mrs. Choate had seen and admired Unter den Linden during a trip to Europe in the early 1890's. After inheriting the estate in the late 1920's, Miss Choate, with the aid of landscape architect, Fletcher Steele, had the original gardens expanded and new features added. The rocks, pedestals, and marble sculptures were gathered by Miss Choate while on a trip to Tokyo in 1935 to attend the annual meeting of the Garden Club of America. Both the house and gardens were opened to the public in 1959.

The formal gardens are tucked on a hillside, with a view westward to the Berkshires. The Afternoon Garden, to the south, glimmers with fountains sprinkling into a black glass pool surrounded by box-edged beds of colored marble pebbles and enclosed by olive trees and clematis-covered Venetian posts. Below, the broad lawn, terraced with banks of ivy and clematis and bor-

dered by Japanese maples and pollarded larch, slopes down to a Chinese pagoda housing a three-hundred-year-old rock on a Ming pedestal that had been in the Summer Palace at Peking. Down the hillside, blue-tiled steps, with fountains on each of four landings, lead through the Birch Grove into the cutting garden. On the upper slope to the north, the Chinese Garden, with a flooring of moss divided by streams running through marble channels, is enclosed by a pink brick wall with a moon gate. Guarded by lions and surrounded by ginkgo trees, its temple houses many Chinese sculptures. On the terraced lower slope, the paths of the Green Garden lead through rows of arborvitae and hemlock hedges into the rose garden. Broad paths of pink marble chips, with beds of roses in the center and at each end, curve down a sloping lawn to a border of tree peonies. In the true Indian meaning of the word, Naumkeag fulfills its name, "Haven of Peace."

THE NEW YORK
BOTANICAL GARDEN

Bronx, New York

Today the garden is world renowned for its research. It has one of the finest horticultural and botanical libraries and herbariums in the Western Hemisphere. Eleven greenhouses display tropical plants, cacti, bromeliaids, and economic plants. Outdoor plantings include a rose garden, rock garden, herb garden, the Montgomery conifer collection, a hemlock forest, and many varieties of trees and flowering shrubs, with irises, narcissi, chrysanthemums, azaleas, and rhododendrons blooming in season.

The garden traces its origin to America's oldest botanical society, The Torrey Botanical Club, and the vision of two of its members, Dr. Nathaniel Lord Britton, professor of botany at Columbia University, and Mrs. Britton, who had visited the Royal Botanical Garden at Kew. Sparked by their enthusiasm, the club proposed that a similar garden be established in New York City. In 1891, the New York Legislature incorporated the New York Botanical Garden and authorized its development on two hundred fifty acres in Bronx Park.

OHME GARDENS

Wenatchee, Washington

Ohme Gardens are perched above a spreading panorama of the Wenatchee Valley, the Columbia River, and the snow-capped Cascade Mountains. When Herman Ohme purchased a small fruit orchard in the valley in 1929, the property included a seven-acre rocky hill covered with sagebrush and desert grass. Impressed by the view above the valley, he began to landscape the rocky outcroppings. From the beginning, he made an effort to avoid the artificial and to stress the natural. He brought native junipers and evergreens from

cacti, and yucca. Within ten years the gardens had attracted many visitors, and at the insistence of friends he opened them to the public in 1939. Since then, he and his son, Gordon, have continued to develop them.

the mountains, built paths through the rocks, made lakes, and planted grass lawns. On the slopes, he planted meadows of dryas, veronica, campanula, dianthus, euphorbia, thyme, vinca, Lewisia tweedyi, hypericum, sagina moss, native ferns,

115

Westbury House, with its lawns, lakes, pools, formal gardens, allées, and trees, reflects the elegance of Long Island estates at the turn of the century. For more than fifty years, it was the home of Mr. and Mrs. John S. Phipps and their family. Mr. Phipps, prominent sportsman and businessman, was the son of Henry Phipps, a partner of Andrew Carnegie. In 1905, the eminent English architect George Crawley designed the Georgian manor house and landscaped the gardens in classical eighteenth-century English style. When Mr. Phipps died in 1958, his will provided that the seventy-acre estate be incorporated as a nonprofit organization and be used for a public museum, botanical garden, and arboretum. A year later, his daughter,

OLD WESTBURY GARDENS

Westbury, Long Island, New York

Mrs. Etienne Boegner, opened the gardens and the house, with its collection of eighteenth-century furniture and paintings, to the public.

Draped in white and yellow roses, the promenade terrace overlooks a broad lawn bordered by a long allée of birches and lindens. In the Boxwood Garden, the columns of the wisteria-covered pergola reflect in a pool surrounded by aged boxwood. In the formal Italian garden, enclosed by a brick wall, phlox, tulips, irises, peonies, poppies, delphiniums, lilies, petunias, hollyhocks, geraniums, dahlias, sunflowers, asters, and chrysanthemums bloom in season. Arbors of roses shade the paths in the sunken circular Rose Garden. Surrounded by woodlands, the still surface of an emerald lake reflects the Georgian mansion on one side and a Roman Temple of Love on the other. Hundreds of ancient trees shade the lawns and paths surrounding the estate.

ORTON PLANTATION GARDENS

Wilmington,

North Carolina

Veiled in an atmosphere of grandeur, Orton Plantation still retains the elegance of its heritage. One would never suspect that its past had ever been interrupted, that Orton had stood abandoned for some twenty years following the Civil War. In 1725, Roger Moore, son of Governor James Moore of South Carolina, settled on the land and called it Orton. Named after the Moore ancestral home in the Lake District of England, Orton became well known as a rice plantation. After the Moore family, Orton was owned by Colonel Benjamin Smith, Governor of North Carolina and one of the founders of the University of North Carolina. In 1840, another owner, Dr. Fredrick Hill, enlarged the house and added the portico with

four large columns. Then, under the ownership of Thomas Miller, Orton survived the Civil War until General Lee's last source of supply was cut off by the fall of nearby Fort Fisher and Fort Anderson. Occupied by the Federalists, Orton became a smallpox hospital. With the bankruptcy of Thomas Miller after the war, combined with the fear that the house had been contaminated, Orton stood deserted until the early 1880's, when Colonel Kenneth Murchinson bought the plantation and restored the house. Colonel Murchinson's son-in-law, James Sprunt, planned and developed the gardens around 1910. Later, his son, Laurence, the present owner of Orton, opened the gardens to the public.

The Orton house, on a high bluff overlooking the Cape Fear River, with a vista of green lawn shaded by pines, magnolias, cedars, and moss-covered live oaks, is surrounded by gardens. Fragrant with camellias from late autumn until late spring, interspersed by wisteria, azalea, dogwood and redbud, roses and flowering cherry, followed by mimosa, bay, crape myrtle, and gardenia, Orton is alive with color throughout the seasons. With the gentle river breezes carrying the call of waterfowl up from the old rice fields and spreading the fragrance of loquat, tea olive, jasmine, osmanthus, and sweet-scented daphne, each in its turn, over the plantation, Orton embodies the charm of the Carolina Low Country.

THE PARK OF ROSES

Columbus, Ohio

One of the finest rose gardens in America, the Park of Roses was created through the combined efforts of the Columbus Rose Club and the Central Ohio Rose Society. In 1947, the Club made a modest proposal for the establishment of a rose garden on the grounds of City Hall. Although the plan was abandoned, the idea sparked the enthusiasm of a newly formed organization, the Central

Ohio Rose Society. A joint committee from both organizations drew up plans for a far more ambitious garden and presented it to the mayor with the appeal, "a rose garden would be valuable as a horticultural research center and as a cultural center for the citizens of the community." In April, 1952, the City Council approved the plan, allotted funds, and created an advisory board—the Columbus Rose Commission. Work began the following month under the supervision of the Division of Parks and Forestry. That fall some two thousand roses were planted, followed by the main plantings in the spring. By June, the garden was completed and opened to the public, with many of the twenty thousand young plants in bloom. The national headquarters of the American Rose Society, which maintains the largest library on rose culture in the world, is nearby.

The garden covers thirty-five acres in Columbus' largest park, Whetstone Park. In a natural setting of gently rolling terrain, meadow, ravine, and woodlands, the hybrid teas, grandifloras, climbers, and floribundas have been planted to blend with one another in color and tone. Today the garden has over thirty-five thousand bushes of more than four hundred and twenty-five varieties.

PHIPPS
CONSERVATORY

Pittsburgh, Pennsylvania

Set among the sloping woodlands of Shenley Park, the thirteen-room conservatory and eight outdoor growing houses were given to the City of Pittsburgh in 1893 by Henry Phipps, a noted philanthropist and steel magnate, who was once a partner of Andrew Carnegie. Between 1936 and 1939, the conservatory was completely renovated, with emphasis on seasonal flower shows rather than the development of plant collections. Although a varied group of exotic plants is still maintained, the conservatory has become well known for its extraordinary flowering plants. It offers classes in plant propagation and a horticultural information service.

The four seasonal shows at the conservatory are displayed in garden settings. Hyacinths, tulips, narcissi, flowering peach, cherry, crab, and almond in the spring are followed by begonias, lilies, and schicanthus in summer. In the fall, chrysanthemums in all varieties and colors are followed by the Christmas show of poinsettias, peppers, and Jerusalem cherries. Outside the conservatory there are fine terraces of herbacious gardens and an azalea garden in a natural setting among old oaks.

123

"SAN SIMEON," THE HEARST ESTATE

San Simeon, California

Rarely, since the day of the Medicis, has an estate existed as grandiose as La Cuesta Enchantada at San Simeon. In 1865, George Hearst, who had made a fortune in mining investments, bought a forty-thousand-acre ranch on the California coast. During the 1870's, he often included his only son, William Randolph, in his informal camping parties at the rustic retreat he had built on the isolated hilltop. After his death, "Camp Hill" passed to his wife, Phoebe Apperson Hearst, and while building his newspaper empire, William Randolph continued to use it as a retreat. On one such visit he wrote to his mother, "As in my youth, I love it here. It is wonderful. I don't want to go back to work and worries." When he inherited the ranch, he immediately began the building of the fabulous

124

estate. For three decades he continued to develop the Moorish style castle and formal garden, enriching them with one of the greatest collections of *objets d'art* in the world. After his death, La Cuesta Enchantada was presented to the people and the State of California by the Hearst Corporation, "in memory of William Randolph Hearst, who created this enchanted hill, and of his mother, who inspired it." It was opened to the public in 1958.

After the garden was planned, Mr. Hearst, determined that it should be developed on the same lavish scale as the castle, had countless wagonloads of rich earth hauled up from the meadow below to replenish the sparse soil on the hill. Overlooking the Pacific Ocean and the mountains, the garden's terraces soon boasted a profusion of flowers and shrubs. Statuesque palms, cedars, and pines complement the formality of marble bas-reliefs, urns, birdbaths, benches, vases, statues, and lights, which ornament the garden.

SANTA BARBARA
BOTANIC GARDEN

Santa Barbara, California

A more perfect setting for the display and study of the native flora of California could not be imagined than Mission Canyon where the Santa Barbara Botanic Garden is located. With a view north to the Santa Ynez Mountains ridged by coulter pines, the garden includes the canyon floor, chaparral-covered slopes, and Mission Creek, where, in 1807, the Franciscan fathers of Mission Santa Barbara built a dam for their water supply. Established in 1926 by a group of garden lovers interested in preserving native California plants, the garden's first acreage was the gift of Mrs. Anna Blaksley in memory of her father, Henry J. Blaksley. In the beginning the fifty-acre garden was affiliated with the Santa Barbara Museum of Natural History, but in 1939 it became an independent organization. Throughout the years, a program of lectures, workshops, and field trips has been developed and a varied research program has been carried on, particularly in the study of the flora of the Santa Barbara Channel Islands.

In early spring the large meadow is a blanket of color with wild strawberries, California poppies, lupines, native buckwheat, wild sage, bush snapdragon, monkey flower, and wild fuchsia, bordered by squawbush, California junipers, and Coast silk-tassel. Circling the meadow, the path is banked by annuals and perennials and shaded by Monterey pine, Coast live oak, California box elder, and Digger pines. Back of the meadow, the path winds up through the Woodland Section of Monterey cypress, redberry, lemonade berry, mountain mahogany, and down the slope covered by currants, gooseberries, hollyleaf cherry, and sugarbush into the Canyon. Protected by big-leaf maples, redwoods, California bay, tanbark oak, and black poplars, the canyon floor is covered with wild blackberry, Douglas nightshade, snowberry, huckleberry, redwood sorrel, and alumroot.

126

The desert cliff rose, the paloverde, Apache plume, sand verbena, white evening primrose, and Joshua tree are among the spring blooming plants in the Desert Section. From late February until May, the Ceanothus Section is in full bloom. With its large plant collection from the Channel Islands, the garden holds interest for the biologist as well as the amateur gardener.

128

SHERWOOD GARDENS

Baltimore, Maryland

One Sunday morning in May, thirty years ago, John Sherwood was surprised to see many uninvited guests enjoying the splendor of his garden. Shortly thereafter, he opened it to the public. Each October some hundred thousand tulips are imported from Holland and a few weeks before they bloom, ten thousand specially grown pansy clumps are planted. For added color there are flowering Japanese cherry, crab apple, pink and white dogwood, lilac, wisteria, and masses of azaleas. In the Bride's Garden, white tulips and pansies highlight the evergreens. The rolling lawns are shaded by old forest trees and evergreens collected from every country in the world. Surrounding the ivy-covered Georgian mansion, patterned after Byrd's "Westover" on the James River, is one of the finest collections of English boxwood in the country.

STERLING FOREST GARDENS

Tuxedo, New York

130

In a woodland over whose trails George Washington led his troops during the Revolution, Sterling Forest Gardens has been created as one of the horticultural showplaces in America. Work began on the gardens in 1958 under the sponsorship of the City Investing Company. Robert W. Dowling, president of the firm, traveled to such famous gardens as Tivoli in Rome, Versailles in France, Kew in England, Keukenhof in Holland, and the gardens of Japan to study their methods of presenting floral displays. Dutch landscape architect Carl van Empelen worked side by side with American landscape architect William Rutherford in planning the garden. Dutch experts were sent by the International Flower Show Committee of the Netherlands to supervise the planting of a million and a half bulbs. Princess Beatrix of the Netherlands inaugurated the planting of the garden by setting the first of these bulbs in place. It was particularly fitting that the people of the Netherlands play such an important role in the development of the one-hundred-twenty-five-acres, for the Dutch were the original settlers of the region. Many of their descendants live there today. The gardens were opened to the public in 1960.

Nestling in a valley of the Ramapo Mountains, among natural woodlands, lakes, and huge rock formations, the garden proper consists of many plantings—a Rose Garden, Terrace Garden, Primrose Garden, Iris Garden, Tulip Garden, Poetry Garden, Annual and Perennial Garden, and a Conservatory Garden. Sterling Forest has the largest single collections of tulips, hyacinths, and daffodils in the United States.

131

STRYBING ARBORETUM AND BOTANICAL GARDEN

San Francisco, California

In a climate of extremes in both temperature and precipitation, the Strybing Arboretum and Botanical Garden grows all the rare and beautiful plants hardy in the section. The arboretum dates back to the 1870's, when William H. Hall, then Superintendent of Golden Gate Park, proposed that twelve acres be set aside for it. With the co-operation of the State Board of Forestry, planting was begun in 1888 by John McLauren, Mr. Hall's successor. In the early 1900's, Mr. McLauren bought many of the exotic plants which had been shown at the Panama Pacific Exposition and had them transplanted to the arboretum. Work on the present forty-acre tract began in late autumn 1937, when Mrs. Helen Strybing left her estate to the Park Commission ". . . for the laying out, establishment, and completion of an arboretum and botanic garden." In 1949, landscape architect Prentice French designed a master plan, which is being carried out by the City and County of San Francisco. A new Garden Center houses the library, and is used for flower shows, educational programs, and meetings of garden clubs.

The plants throughout the arboretum are arranged according to their geographic origin. Winding paths lead through sections of trees and plants from Japan, Australia, South Africa, Mexico, China, South America, and the Mediterranean. Masses of flowers and shrubs surround the large section of native California trees.

In the age-old tradition of the Chinese, originators of botanic gardens, the late Colonel Boyce Thompson stated the purpose of his arboretum: ". . . to collect all the plants of the desert countries and find their practical use for the benefit of mankind." The site, first farmed by Apache Indians and then by homesteaders, was familiar territory to Colonel Thompson. On horseback, he had often ridden through Queen Creek Canyon from Superior to Miami to visit his mining properties. Upon his retirement in 1923, he built his winter home atop Picket Post Mountain overlooking the Canyon. While planting his grounds, he became interested in the local vegetation and decided to explore the possibilities of creating a research center for the study of plants of the arid and sub-arid regions. After consulting leading Southwestern horticul-

BOYCE THOMPSON
SOUTHWESTERN ARBORETUM

Superior, Arizona

turalists, he established the arboretum in 1924 and opened it to the public in 1929. Today, it is a source of desert-plant research material for chemists, drug manufacturers, and botanists. It has a free international seed-exchange service.

The arboretum, at the foot of the Pinal Mountains, is surrounded by high peaks, deep canyons, rugged crags, rolling hills, and level mesas. Almond, olive, Natal plum, jujube, pomegranate, persimmon, pistachio, walnut, and pineapple guava trees cast their green and bear their fruit against the red-tinged canyon. In the wildflower section, desert marigolds, evening primroses, desert sunflowers, poppies, and pentstemons shed their glow over the canyon floor. In the eucalyptus grove, red box, sugar gum, gray ironbark, coral gum, and desert mallee shade the myrtle, honey-bush, mesquite, lysiloma, and ostemoeles. Along Desert Walk, varieties of yucca, agave, Furcraea, cholla, and aloes outline the barrenness of the mountains.

134

UNIVERSITY OF CALIFORNIA BOTANICAL GARDEN

Berkeley, California

In 1892, twenty-four years after its charter had been signed, the University started its botanical garden on a plot near the center of the campus.

In 1928, the garden was moved to its present site in Strawberry Canyon overlooking San Francisco Bay—for scenic beauty as well as the excellent growing conditions provided by air currents from the Pacific Ocean which alleviate extremes in climate. The garden is noted for its various geographical units which have been collected during several plant-hunting expeditions by faculty members. On the first of these, in 1931, Dr. Joseph Rock traveled through Tibet and western China and returned with some one thousand rhododendron species to add to the collection in Rhododendron Dell. Many of the plants in the succulent garden were gathered by Dr. T. H. Goodspeed during expeditions to the Andean region of South America, which he directed from 1936 until 1958. The garden's primary function is to provide teaching and research facilities for university students interested in botany and landscape architecture.

On the upper slope, the odd-shaped and bright blossoming succulents are landscaped among rocks and backed by trees and plants from Africa. The meadow is aglow in the spring with native California plants. Trees and plants from South America, Australia, New Zealand, and Hawaii are set in individual areas. Throughout the greenhouses there are fine collections of orchids, ferns, geraniums, and fuchsia, as well as tropical plants. The Herb Garden is maintained in co-operation with the Herb Society of America.

UNIVERSITY OF WASHINGTON ARBORETUM

Seattle, Washington

The soil, climate, and location of the arboretum enable it to grow one of the largest selections of plant materials in the United States north of the subtropical areas. The first arboretum at the University dates back to 1894, but the present one, of two hundred fifty acres, was established in 1935 by the University's Board of Regents and Seattle's Board of Park Commissioners. The first director, Dean Hugo Winkenwerder of the College of Forestry, set as the arboretum's aim, ". . . to organize and sustain an arboretum for the benefit of local citizens, students, and everyone living in the Northwest." Under the sponsorship of the Seattle Garden Club, the arboretum was designed by the noted landscape architects, the Olmsted Brothers, in 1936. The basic construction was done by the WPA. Donations of two large rhododendron

groupings, by Dr. Cecil Tenny in 1937 and Mr. Charles O. Dexter in 1938, formed the nucleus of the large collection. During the past twenty years, hundreds of new and rare plants have been introduced by the arboretum. It offers classes in plant propagation, botany, and plant materials, as well as horticultural and botanical information services and the use of a reference library of books, slides, and photographs.

The arboretum is at the edge of Lake Washington, and its trails and roads wind around other lakes, through valleys, and up hillsides. Of its five hundred species of trees more than four hundred are native to other climates. Beginning in January and ending in December, there is a succession of seasonal bloom from the early camellias through the azaleas and rhododendrons to the hollies and Washington and Lavelle thorns.

WASHINGTON PARK

Denver, Colorado

Appropriately, Washington Park has both a Martha Washington Garden and a scion of the old elm under which George Washington took command of the Continental Army in 1775 in Cambridge, Massachusetts. One of Denver's largest parks, its one hundred sixty-five acres were given to the city by various donors between 1899 and 1908. The gardens are under the supervision of the Park Department and the flowers are supplied by the department's greenhouses. The park with rolling, tree-shaded lawns, gardens, and lakes has a view to the peaks of the Rockies. Overlooking one lake, the Martha Washington Garden is an exact replica of one at Mount Vernon which was designed by George Washington. The formal beds of early blooming perennials and summer annuals are bordered by dwarf hedges of lodense privet. Magnolias, fruit trees, and lilacs add fragrance. Hollyhocks, lilies, and native wildflowers cluster among the herbs in the rock garden bordering on a small pond. In the sunken informal garden, beds of irises, peonies, petunias, marigolds, feverfew, pinks, phlox, asters, geraniums, snapdragons, salvias, gladioli, dahlias, and chrysanthemums are designed to give both variation and balance in color and form.

141

WINTERTHUR

Wilmington, Delaware

Winterthur combines one of the richest collections of furniture and one of the finest gardens in America today. The estate dates back to 1837 when James Bidermann bought some four hundred forty-five acres of land in Christiana Hundred, New Castle County. Two years later, while on a trip to Europe with his wife, the former Evelina du Pont, Mr. Bidermann had a French architect draw up plans for his house, which he named "Winterthur," after his home in Switzerland. Upon his death in 1865, his son, James Irénée Bidermann, inherited Winterthur and two years later sold it to his mother's brother, Henry du Pont. His son, Henry Junior, a Civil War winner of the Congressional Medal of Honor, inherited Winterthur in 1889. Upon his death in 1926, the estate passed on to his son, Henry Francis du Pont, who for twenty-five years devoted his time to developing the gardens and assembling the largest collection of early American furniture and decorative arts ever brought together. In 1951, he deeded the estate to the Winterthur Corporation, an educational and charitable foundation. In that same year it was opened to the public.

142

Mr. du Pont himself designed the gardens, in which the flowers have been nurtured in a natural environment of meadows, fields, and woodlands. Tanbark walks and turf paths wander across lawns banked with azaleas, through woodlands protecting delicate wildflowers and ferns, through open dales of rhododendron and tree peonies, across meadows of daffodils and narcissi bordered by azaleas and shaded by old oaks and poplars. Though now only a visitor, Mr. du Pont says he is still head gardener.

WOODLAND PARK
ROSE GARDEN

Sitting high on a ridge above the flow of shipping on Puget Sound, Woodland Park Rose Garden overlooks the heart of Seattle. The garden was originally created by Guy Phinney, an Englishman who moved west from Nova Scotia in the late 1800's and bought one hundred seventy-nine acres of forest land. Designing it as an English park, Mr. Phinney built a house on the upper part of the property and planted formal gardens around it; on the lower part he raised imported deer. He opened the park to the public and built a private trolley to transport visitors around it. His plans for further development came to an end when he suffered financial losses during the Panic of 1893. The park had been used as a camp by the U.S. Cavalry in 1888 and the following year as a stop-

over for Laplanders on their way to Alaska. In 1900, the City of Seattle purchased Phinney Park, but it stood deserted until 1922, when the Seattle Rose Society and the Seattle Lions Club suggested that the Park Department develop it into a rose garden. From contributions, both organizations donated the first rose plantings. Today, it is a demonstration garden for the American Rose Society and the All-American Rose Selections.

Edging on Green Lake in the park, the garden is surrounded by pines, cedars, spruces, and firs. The pools, fountains, and arbors of roses throughout the garden add to its informal design. The fifty-two hundred rose bushes include one hundred ninety varieties of floribundas, hybrid teas, and grandifloras. Located in one of the most suitable climates in the United States for rose culture, Woodland Park delights all garden lovers.

INDEX

148